Graphing Equations

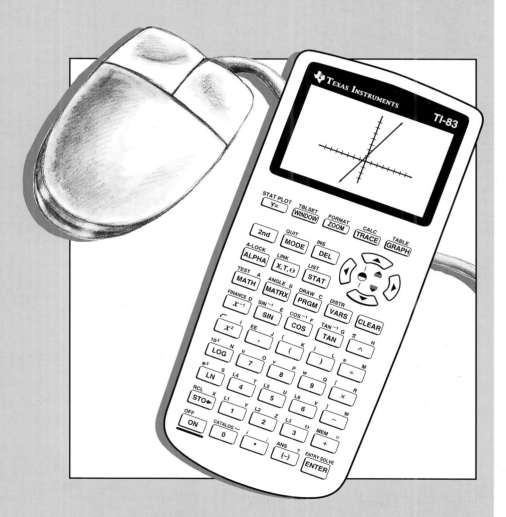

Britannica

ENCYCLOPÆDIA BRITANNICA EDUCATIONAL CORPORATION

Mathematics in Context is a comprehensive curriculum for the middle grades. It was developed in collaboration with the Wisconsin Center for Education Research, School of Education, University of Wisconsin–Madison and the Freudenthal Institute at the University of Utrecht, The Netherlands, with the support of National Science Foundation Grant No. 9054928.

National Science Foundation

Opinions expressed are those of the authors
and not necessarily those of the Foundation

ISBN 0-7826-1549-X
1 2 3 4 5 WK 02 01 00 99 98

The *Mathematics in Context* Development Team

Mathematics in Context is a comprehensive curriculum for the middle grades. The National Science Foundation funded the National Center for Research in Mathematical Sciences Education at the University of Wisconsin–Madison to develop and field-test the materials from 1991 through 1996. The Freudenthal Institute at the University of Utrecht in The Netherlands, as a subcontractor, collaborated with the University of Wisconsin–Madison on the development of the curriculum.

The initial version of *Graphing Equations* was developed by Martin Kindt and Monica Wijers. It was adapted for use in American schools by Mary S. Spence, Laura J. Brinker, Margaret A. Pligge, and Jack Burrill.

National Center for Research in Mathematical Sciences Education Staff

Thomas A. Romberg
Director

Joan Daniels Pedro
Assistant to the Director

Gail Burrill
Coordinator
Field Test Materials

Margaret R. Meyer
Coordinator
Pilot Test Materials

Mary Ann Fix
Editorial Coordinator

Sherian Foster
Editorial Coordinator

James A. Middleton
Pilot Test Coordinator

Margaret A. Pligge
First Edition Coordinator

Project Staff

Jonathan Brendefur
Laura J. Brinker
James Browne
Jack Burrill
Rose Byrd
Peter Christiansen
Barbara Clarke
Doug Clarke
Beth R. Cole

Fae Dremock
Jasmina Milinkovic
Kay Schultz
Mary C. Shafer
Julia A. Shew
Aaron N. Simon
Marvin Smith
Stephanie Z. Smith
Mary S. Spence
Kathleen A. Steele

Freudenthal Institute Staff

Jan de Lange
Director

Els Feijs
Coordinator

Martin van Reeuwijk
Coordinator

Project Staff

Mieke Abels
Nina Boswinkel
Frans van Galen
Koeno Gravemeijer
Marja van den Heuvel-Panhuizen
Jan Auke de Jong
Vincent Jonker
Ronald Keijzer

Martin Kindt
Jansie Niehaus
Nanda Querelle
Anton Roodhardt
Leen Streefland
Adri Treffers
Monica Wijers
Astrid de Wild

Acknowledgments

Several school districts used and evaluated one or more versions of the materials: Ames Community School District, Ames, Iowa; Parkway School District, Chesterfield, Missouri; Stoughton Area School District, Stoughton, Wisconsin; Madison Metropolitan School District, Madison, Wisconsin; Milwaukee Public Schools, Milwaukee, Wisconsin; and Dodgeville School District, Dodgeville, Wisconsin. Two sites were involved in staff developments as well as formative evaluation of materials: Culver City, California, and Memphis, Tennessee. Two sites were developed through partnership with Encyclopædia Britannica Educational Corporation: Miami, Florida, and Puerto Rico. University Partnerships were developed with mathematics educators who worked with preservice teachers to familiarize them with the curriculum and to obtain their advice on the curriculum materials. The materials were also used at several other schools throughout the United States.

We at Encyclopædia Britannica Educational Corporation extend our thanks to all who had a part in making this program a success. Some of the participants instrumental in the program's development are as follows:

Allapattah Middle School
Miami, Florida
Nemtalla (Nikolai) Barakat

Ames Middle School
Ames, Iowa
Kathleen Coe
Judd Freeman
Gary W. Schnieder
Ronald H. Stromen
Lyn Terrill

Bellerive Elementary
Creve Coeur, Missouri
Judy Hetterscheidt
Donna Lohman
Gary Alan Nunn
Jakke Tchang

Brookline Public Schools
Brookline, Massachusetts
Rhonda K. Weinstein
Deborah Winkler

Cass Middle School
Milwaukee, Wisconsin
Tami Molenda
Kyle F. Witty

Central Middle School
Waukesha, Wisconsin
Nancy Reese

Craigmont Middle School
Memphis, Tennessee
Sharon G. Ritz
Mardest K. VanHooks

Crestwood Elementary
Madison, Wisconsin
Diane Hein
John Kalson

Culver City Middle School
Culver City, California
Marilyn Culbertson
Joel Evans
Joy Ellen Kitzmiller
Patricia R. O'Connor
Myrna Ann Perks, Ph.D.
David H. Sanchez
John Tobias
Kelley Wilcox

Cutler Ridge Middle School
Miami, Florida
Lorraine A. Valladares

Dodgeville Middle School
Dodgeville, Wisconsin
Jacqueline A. Kamps
Carol Wolf

Edwards Elementary
Ames, Iowa
Diana Schmidt

Fox Prairie Elementary
Stoughton, Wisconsin
Tony Hjelle

Grahamwood Elementary
Memphis, Tennessee
M. Lynn McGoff
Alberta Sullivan

Henry M. Flagler Elementary
Miami, Florida
Frances R. Harmon

Horning Middle School
Waukesha, Wisconsin
Connie J. Marose
Thomas F. Clark

Huegel Elementary
Madison, Wisconsin
Nancy Brill
Teri Hedges
Carol Murphy

Hutchison Middle School
Memphis, Tennessee
Maria M. Burke
Vicki Fisher
Nancy D. Robinson

Idlewild Elementary
Memphis, Tennessee
Linda Eller

Jefferson Elementary
Santa Ana, California
Lydia Romero-Cruz

Jefferson Middle School
Madison, Wisconsin
Jane A. Beebe
Catherine Buege
Linda Grimmer
John Grueneberg
Nancy Howard
Annette Porter
Stephen H. Sprague
Dan Takkunen
Michael J. Vena

Jesus Sanabria Cruz School
Yabucoa, Puerto Rico
Andreíta Santiago Serrano

John Muir Elementary School
Madison, Wisconsin
Julie D'Onofrio
Jane M. Allen-Jauch
Kent Wells

Kegonsa Elementary
Stoughton, Wisconsin
Mary Buchholz
Louisa Havlik
Joan Olsen
Dominic Weisse

Linwood Howe Elementary
Culver City, California
Sandra Checel
Ellen Thireos

Mitchell Elementary
Ames, Iowa
Henry Gray
Matt Ludwig

New School of Northern Virginia
Fairfax, Virginia
Denise Jones

Northwood Elementary
Ames, Iowa
Eleanor M. Thomas

Orchard Ridge Elementary
Madison, Wisconsin
Mary Paquette
Carrie Valentine

Parkway West Middle School
Chesterfield, Missouri
Elissa Aiken
Ann Brenner
Gail R. Smith

Ridgeway Elementary
Ridgeway, Wisconsin
Lois Powell
Florence M. Wasley

Roosevelt Elementary
Ames, Iowa
Linda A. Carver

Roosevelt Middle
Milwaukee, Wisconsin
Sandra Simmons

Ross Elementary
Creve Coeur, Missouri
Annette Isselhard
Sheldon B. Korklan
Victoria Linn
Kathy Stamer

St. Joseph's School
Dodgeville, Wisconsin
Rita Van Dyck
Sharon Wimer

St. Maarten Academy
St. Peters, St. Maarten, NA
Shareed Hussain

Sarah Scott Middle School
Milwaukee, Wisconsin
Kevin Haddon

Sawyer Elementary
Ames, Iowa
Karen Bush Hoiberg

Sennett Middle School
Madison, Wisconsin
Brenda Abitz
Lois Bell
Shawn M. Jacobs

Sholes Middle School
Milwaukee, Wisconsin
Chris Gardner
Ken Haddon

Stephens Elementary
Madison, Wisconsin
Katherine Hogan
Shirley M. Steinbach
Kathleen H. Vegter

Stoughton Middle School
Stoughton, Wisconsin
Sally Bertelson
Polly Goepfert
Jacqueline M. Harris
Penny Vodak

Toki Middle School
Madison, Wisconsin
Gail J. Anderson
Vicky Grice
Mary M. Ihlenfeldt
Steve Jernegan
Jim Leidel
Theresa Loehr
Maryann Stephenson
Barbara Takkunen
Carol Welsch

Trowbridge Elementary
Milwaukee, Wisconsin
Jacqueline A. Nowak

W. R. Thomas Middle School
Miami, Florida
Michael Paloger

Wooddale Elementary Middle School
Memphis, Tennessee
Velma Quinn Hodges
Jacqueline Marie Hunt

Yahara Elementary
Stoughton, Wisconsin
Mary Bennett
Kevin Wright

Site Coordinators

Mary L. Delagardelle—Ames Community Schools, Ames, Iowa

Dr. Hector Hirigoyen—Miami, Florida

Audrey Jackson—Parkway School District, Chesterfield, Missouri

Jorge M. López—Puerto Rico

Susan Militello—Memphis, Tennessee

Carol Pudlin—Culver City, California

Reviewers and Consultants

Michael N. Bleicher
Professor of Mathematics
University of Wisconsin–Madison
Madison, WI

Diane J. Briars
Mathematics Specialist
Pittsburgh Public Schools
Pittsburgh, PA

Donald Chambers
Director of Dissemination
University of Wisconsin–Madison
Madison, WI

Don W. Collins
Assistant Professor of Mathematics Education
Western Kentucky University
Bowling Green, KY

Joan Elder
Mathematics Consultant
Los Angeles Unified School District
Los Angeles, CA

Elizabeth Fennema
Professor of Curriculum and Instruction
University of Wisconsin–Madison
Madison, WI

Nancy N. Gates
University of Memphis
Memphis, TN

Jane Donnelly Gawronski
Superintendent
Escondido Union High School
Escondido, CA

M. Elizabeth Graue
Assistant Professor of Curriculum and Instruction
University of Wisconsin–Madison
Madison, WI

Jodean E. Grunow
Consultant
Wisconsin Department of Public Instruction
Madison, WI

John G. Harvey
Professor of Mathematics and Curriculum & Instruction
University of Wisconsin–Madison
Madison, WI

Simon Hellerstein
Professor of Mathematics
University of Wisconsin–Madison
Madison, WI

Elaine J. Hutchinson
Senior Lecturer
University of Wisconsin–Stevens Point
Stevens Point, WI

Richard A. Johnson
Professor of Statistics
University of Wisconsin–Madison
Madison, WI

James J. Kaput
Professor of Mathematics
University of Massachusetts–Dartmouth
Dartmouth, MA

Richard Lehrer
Professor of Educational Psychology
University of Wisconsin–Madison
Madison, WI

Richard Lesh
Professor of Mathematics
University of Massachusetts–Dartmouth
Dartmouth, MA

Mary M. Lindquist
Callaway Professor of Mathematics Education
Columbus College
Columbus, GA

Baudilio (Bob) Mora
Coordinator of Mathematics & Instructional Technology
Carrollton-Farmers Branch Independent School District
Carrollton, TX

Paul Trafton
Professor of Mathematics
University of Northern Iowa
Cedar Falls, IA

Norman L. Webb
Research Scientist
University of Wisconsin–Madison
Madison, WI

Paul H. Williams
Professor of Plant Pathology
University of Wisconsin–Madison
Madison, WI

Linda Dager Wilson
Assistant Professor
University of Delaware
Newark, DE

Robert L. Wilson
Professor of Mathematics
University of Wisconsin–Madison
Madison, WI

Contents

Dear Teacher,

Welcome! *Mathematics in Context* is designed to reflect the National Council of Teachers of Mathematics Standards for School Mathematics and to ground mathematical content in a variety of real-world contexts. Rather than relying on you to explain and demonstrate generalized definitions, rules, or algorithms, students investigate questions directly related to a particular context and construct mathematical understanding and meaning from that context.

The curriculum encompasses 10 units per grade level. *Graphing Equations* is the first in the algebra strand for grade 8/9, to be used after the grade 7/8 algebra units *Ups and Downs* and *Decision Making,* and the grade 7/8 geometry unit *Looking at an Angle.* The unit also lends itself to independent use–to introduce students to experiences that will enrich their understanding of the linear relationship, represented by graphs and by equations. Many of the grade 8/9 units in all four strands build on *Graphing Equations.* Therefore it is recommended that you do this unit at the beginning of the year.

In addition to the Teacher Guide and Student Books, *Mathematics in Context* offers the following components that will inform and support your teaching:

- *Teacher Resource and Implementation Guide,* which provides an overview of the complete system, including program implementation, philosophy, and rationale

- *Number Tools,* Volumes 1 and 2, which are a series of blackline masters that serve as review sheets or practice pages involving number issues and basic skills

- *News in Numbers,* which is a set of additional activities that can be inserted between or within other units; it includes a number of measurement problems that require estimation.

Thank you for choosing *Mathematics in Context.* We wish you success and inspiration!

Sincerely,

The Mathematics in Context Development Team

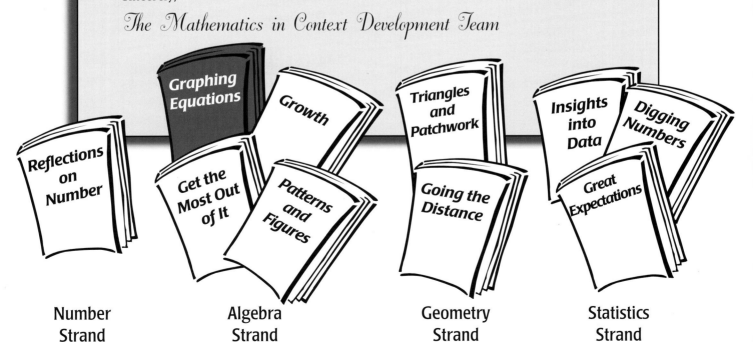

Number Strand   Algebra Strand   Geometry Strand   Statistics Strand

Overview

BRITANNICA

Mathematics in Context

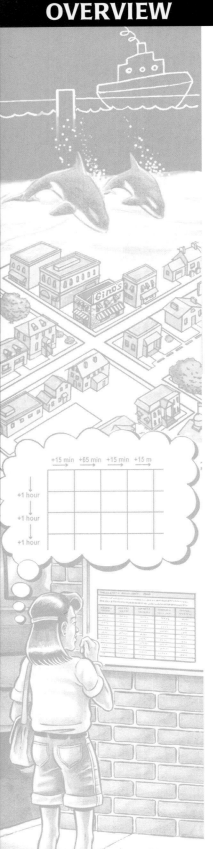

How to Use This Book

This unit is one of 40 for the middle grades. Each unit can be used independently; however, the 40 units are designed to make up a complete, connected curriculum (10 units per grade level). There is a Student Book and a Teacher Guide for each unit.

Each Teacher Guide comprises elements that assist the teacher in the presentation of concepts and in understanding the general direction of the unit and the program as a whole. Becoming familiar with this structure will make using the units easier.

Each Teacher Guide consists of six basic parts:

- Overview
- Student Materials and Teaching Notes
- Assessment Activities and Solutions
- Glossary
- Blackline Masters
- Try This! Solutions

Overview

Before beginning this unit, read the Overview in order to understand the purpose of the unit and to develop strategies for facilitating instruction. The Overview provides helpful information about the unit's focus, pacing, goals, and assessment, as well as explanations about how the unit fits with the rest of the *Mathematics in Context* curriculum.

Student Materials and Teaching Notes

This Teacher Guide contains all of the student pages (except the Try This! activities), each of which faces a page of solutions, samples of students' work, and hints and comments about how to facilitate instruction. Note: Solutions for the Try This! activities can be found at the back of this Teacher Guide.

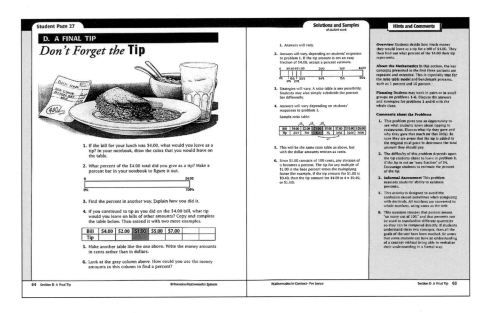

Each section within the unit begins with a two-page spread that describes the work students do, the goals of the section, new vocabulary, and materials needed, as well as providing information about the mathematics in the section and ideas for pacing, planning instruction, homework, and assessment.

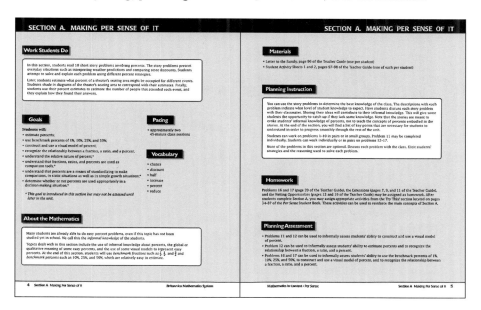

Assessment Activities and Solutions

Information about assessment can be found in several places in this Teacher Guide. General information about assessment is given in the Overview; informal assessment opportunities are identified on the teacher pages that face each student page; and the Assessment Activities section of this guide provides formal assessment opportunities.

Glossary

The Glossary defines all vocabulary words listed on the Section Opener pages. It includes the mathematical terms that may be new to students, as well as words associated with the contexts introduced in the unit. (Note: The Student Book does not have a glossary. This allows students to construct their own definitions, based on their personal experiences with the unit activities.)

Blackline Masters

At the back of this Teacher Guide are blackline masters for photocopying. The blackline masters include a letter to families (to be sent home with students before beginning the unit), several student activity sheets, and assessment masters.

Try This! Solutions

Also included in the back of this Teacher Guide are the solutions to several Try This! activities—one related to each section of the unit—that can be used to reinforce the unit's main concepts. The Try This! activities are located in the back of the Student Book.

Unit Focus

The heart of this unit is the study of lines. Students graph linear relationships and study linear equations. Two coordinate systems, the Cartesian and polar systems, are an important part of the unit, as is students' use of the graphing calculator. The graphing calculator is used as a tool to graph lines and find an equation for a drawn line.

In this unit, algebra is connected to geometry. The angle and its tangent ratio are used to build students' understanding of the concept of slope. The relationship between the equation of the line in slope-intercept form ($y = i + sx$) and its graph is made explicit.

The intersection of two lines is investigated in different ways: visually, using a model that is later transformed into the number line; algebraically, by doing the same operation on both sides of the equals sign; and with the use of graphs. Variables and unknowns play an important role in the unit and the notation of x and y is made more formal.

Mathematical Content

- describing directions using angles and wind directions
- graphing points and lines in the coordinate plane
- understanding the slope and tangent ratio of a line
- understanding the meaning of the y-intercept
- recognizing parallel lines
- creating the equation of a line
- solving single-variable linear equations
- finding the point of intersection of two lines

Prior Knowledge

This unit assumes students can do the following:

- add, subtract, multiply, and divide rational numbers in all representations (decimals, percentages, fractions)
- use metric measurements
- graph lines (as introduced and used in the unit *Ups and Downs*)
- read and use compass directions and measure angles with a compass card or protractor (as in the units *Figuring All the Angles* and the *Looking at an Angle*)
- read and use coordinates on a coordinate grid (as in the units *Operations* and *Ups and Downs*)
- understand inequality notation (as in the units *Operations* and *Decision Making*)
- read simple formulas relating two variables (as in the units *Building Formulas* and *Ups and Downs*)

In addition, it is helpful if students can:

- find the tangent of an angle (as in *Looking at an Angle*)
- use a graphing calculator to draw a line

This unit should be taught after the units *Decision Making, Ups and Downs, Building Formulas,* and *Looking at an Angle.*

Planning and Preparation
Pacing: 13–17 days

Section	Work Students Do	Pacing*	Materials
A. Where There's Smoke	■ use wind directions and angles to locate forest fires	1–2 days	■ Letter to the Family (one per student) ■ Student Activity Sheets 1–3 (one of each per student) ■ local area or park maps, optional (one per student) ■ rulers (one per student) ■ compass cards (one per student) ■ protractors, optional (one per student)
B. Coordinates on a Screen	■ use coordinates to locate fires ■ use and draw horizontal and vertical lines ■ use equations that correspond to horizontal and vertical lines	2–3 days	■ Student Activity Sheet 4 (one per student) ■ see page 19 for the Teacher Guide for a complete list of the materials and quantities needed
C. Directions as Pairs of Numbers	■ use horizontal and vertical moves to give directions ■ find the slope of lines ■ graph lines	2–3 days	■ Student Activity Sheets 5 and 6 (one of each per student) ■ rulers (one per student) ■ graph paper, optional (one sheet per student)
D. An Equation of a Line	■ work with equations of lines, intercepts, and slopes ■ graph equations	3 days	■ see page 55 of the Teacher Guide for a complete list of the materials and quantities needed
E. Solving Equations	■ solve equations of the form $a + bx = c + dx$ algebraically	3–4 days	■ see page 73 of the Teacher Guide for a complete list of the materials and quantities needed
F. Intersecting Lines	■ graph two separate lines and find the point of intersection	2 days	■ graphing calculators (one per student) ■ graph paper (one sheet per student)

* One day is approximately equivalent to one 45-minute class session.

Preparation

In the *Teacher Resource and Implementation Guide* is an extensive description of the philosophy underlying both the content and the pedagogy of the *Mathematics in Context* curriculum. Suggestions for preparation are also given in the Hints and Comments columns of this Teacher Guide. You may want to consider the following:

- Work through the unit before teaching it. If possible, take on the role of the student and discuss your strategies with other teachers.

- Use the overhead projector for student demonstrations, particularly with overhead transparencies of the student activity sheets and any manipulatives used in the unit.

- Invite students to use drawings and examples to illustrate and clarify their answers.

- Allow students to work at different levels of sophistication. Some students may need concrete materials, while others can work at a more abstract level.

- Provide opportunities and support for students to share their strategies, which often differ. This allows students to take part in class discussions and introduces them to alternative ways to think about the mathematics in the unit.

- In some cases, it may be necessary to read the problems to students or to pair students to facilitate their understanding of the printed materials.

- A list of the materials needed for this unit is in the chart on page xiii.

- Try to follow the recommended pacing chart on page xiii. You can easily spend much more time on this unit than the number of class periods indicated. Bear in mind, however, that many of the topics introduced in this unit will be revisited and covered more thoroughly in other *Mathematics in Context* units.

Resources

For Teachers

Books and Magazines
- Stenmark, Jean Kerr, ed. *Mathematics Assessment: Myths, Models, Good Questions, and Practical Suggestions* (Reston, Virginia: The National Council of Teachers of Mathematics, Inc., 1991)
- Sandwehr, James, and Watkins. *Exploring Data* (Palo Alto, CA: Dale Seymour Publications, 1995)

Assessment

Planning Assessment

In keeping with the NCTM Assessment Standards, valid assessment should be based on evidence drawn from several sources. (See the full discussion of assessment philosophies in the *Teacher Resource and Implementation Guide.*) An assessment plan for this unit may draw from the following sources:

- Observations—look, listen, and record observable behavior.

- Interactive Responses—in a teacher-facilitated situation, note how students respond, clarify, revise, and extend their thinking.

- Products—look for the quality of thought evident in student projects, test answers, worksheet solutions, or writings.

These categories are not meant to be mutually exclusive. In fact, observation is a key part in assessing interactive responses and also key to understanding the end results of projects and writings.

Ongoing Assessment Opportunities

- **Problems within Sections**
  To evaluate ongoing progress, *Mathematics in Context* identifies informal assessment opportunities and the goals that these particular problems assess throughout the Teacher Guide. There are also indications as to what you might expect from your students.

- **Section Summary Questions**
  The summary questions at the end of each section are vehicles for informal assessment (see Teacher Guide pages 16, 34, 52, 70, 92, and 102).

End-of-Unit Assessment Opportunities

In the back of this Teacher Guide, there are two assessment activities that require about two 45-minute class periods. For a more detailed description of these assessment activities, see the Assessment Overview (Teacher Guide pages 104 and 105). You may want to use problems from the sections in addition to these end-of-unit assessments to get a complete picture of students' understanding of the mathematics in the unit.

You may also wish to design your own culminating project. For more assessment ideas, refer to the charts on pages xvi and xvii.

Goals and Assessment

In the *Mathematics in Context* curriculum, unit goals, categorized according to cognitive procedures, relate to the strand goals and to the NCTM Curriculum and Evaluation Standards. Additional information about these goals is found in the *Teacher Resource and Implementation Guide*. The *Mathematics in Context* curriculum is designed to help students develop their abilities so that they can perform with understanding in each of the categories listed below. It is important to note that the attainment of goals in one category is not a prerequisite to attaining those in another category. In fact, students should progress simultaneously toward several goals in different categories.

	Goal	Ongoing Assessment Opportunities	End-of-Unit Assessment Opportunities
Conceptual and Procedural Knowledge	**1.** describe and graph directions using wind directions and angles	**Section A** p. 16, #9	Treasure Island, p. 122, #1, #2
	2. understand and graph horizontal and vertical lines and their equations	**Section B** p. 30, #13 p. 34, #17, #18, #19	
	3. use inequalities to describe regions restricted by horizontal and vertical lines	**Section B** p. 30, #13	Treasure Island, p. 123, #6, #8
	4. find and use equations of the form $y = i + sx$ using the slope and y-intercept	**Section D** p. 60, #8 p. 64, #13, #14 p. 70, #24, #25 **Section F** p. 100, #11 p. 102, #12, #13	Rent a Car, p. 121, #3, #4, #8 Treasure Island, p. 122, #1, #2, p. 123, #7
	5. graph equations of the form $y = i + sx$	**Section D** p. 70, #25 **Section F** p. 98, #5, #6 p. 102, #12, #13	Rent a Car, p. 121, #6 Treasure Island, p. 122, #3 p. 123, #7
	6. solve equations of the form $a + bx = c + dx$	**Section E** p. 82, #13 p. 88, #19–#21 p. 92, #24, #25 **Section F** p. 98, #5, #6 p. 100, #11 p. 102, #12, #13	Rent a Car, p. 121, #5 Treasure Island, p. 122, #4 p. 123, #7

	Goal	Ongoing Assessment Opportunities		End-of-Unit Assessment Opportunities
Reasoning, Communicating, Thinking, and Making Connections	**7.** understand the meaning of slope in different contexts	**Section C**	p. 44, #12 p. 48, #17, #18 p. 50, #19 p. 52, #20, #21	Treasure Island, p. 122, #4 p. 123, #7
		Section F	p. 102, #13	
	8. understand how to find the intersection point of two lines, algebraically and graphically	**Section A** **Section F**	p. 10, #4 p. 98, #5, #6 p. 100, #8 p. 100, #11 p. 102, #12, #13	Treasure Island, p. 122, #1, #2 p. 123, #7
	9. understand the graph of a line in the coordinate plane	**Section B**	p. 34, #17, #18, #19	Rent a Car, p. 121, #7, #8 Treasure Island, p. 122, #3 p. 123, #7
		Section C	p. 48, #17, #18 p. 50, #19 p. 52, #20, #21	
		Section D **Section F**	p. 70, #25 p. 100, #11 p. 102, #12, #13	

	Goal	Ongoing Assessment Opportunities		End-of-Unit Assessment Opportunities
Modeling, Nonroutine Problem-Solving, Critically Analyzing, and Generalizing	**10.** model a problem situation and translate it to a graph or an equation	**Section E**	p. 88, #19 p. 92, #25	Rent a Car, p. 121, #4
		Section F	p. 102, #12	
	11. choose an appropriate way to solve equations	**Section E** **Section F**	p. 92, #24, #25 p. 100, #11 p. 102, #12, #13	Treasure Island, p. 123, #7
	12. understand the similarities between graphic and algebraic strategies	**Section F**	p. 100, #11 p. 102, #12, #13	Rent a Car, p. 121, #7

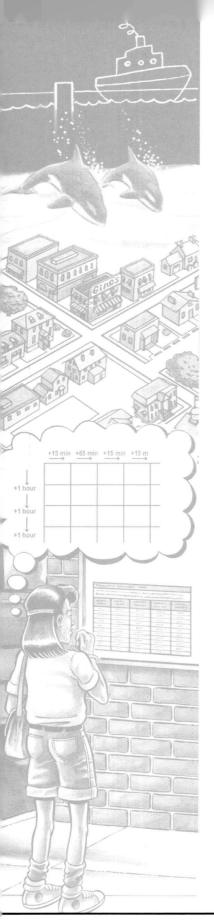

More about Assessment

Scoring and Analyzing Assessment Responses

Students may respond to assessment questions with various levels of mathematical sophistication and elaboration. Each student's response should be considered for the mathematics that it shows, and not judged on whether or not it includes an expected response. Responses to some of the assessment questions may be viewed as either correct or incorrect, but many answers will need flexible judgment by the teacher. Descriptive judgments related to specific goals and partial credit often provide more helpful feedback than percentage scores.

Openly communicate your expectations to all students, and report achievement and progress for each student relative to those expectations. When scoring students' responses, try to think about how they are progressing toward the goals of the unit and the strand.

Student Portfolios

Generally, a portfolio is a collection of student-selected pieces that is representative of a student's work. A portfolio may include evaluative comments by you or by the student. See the *Teacher Resource and Implementation Guide* for more ideas on portfolio focus and use.

A comprehensive discussion about the contents, management, and evaluation of portfolios can be found in *Mathematics Assessment: Myths, Models, Good Questions, and Practical Suggestions,* pp. 35–48.

Student Self-Evaluation

Self-evaluation encourages students to reflect on their progress in learning mathematical concepts, their developing abilities to use mathematics, and their dispositions toward mathematics. The following examples illustrate ways to incorporate student self-evaluations as one component of your assessment plan.

- Ask students to comment, in writing, on each piece they have chosen for their portfolios and on the progress they see in the pieces overall.
- Give a writing assignment entitled "What I Know Now about [a math concept] and What I Think about It." This will give you information about each student's disposition toward mathematics as well as his or her knowledge.
- Interview individuals or small groups to elicit what they have learned, what they think is important, and why.

Suggestions for self-inventories can be found in *Mathematics Assessment: Myths, Models, Good Questions, and Practical Suggestions,* pp. 55–58.

Summary Discussion

Discuss specific lessons and activities in the unit—what the student learned from them and what the activities have in common. This can be done in whole-class discussion, in small groups, or in personal interviews.

Connections across the *Mathematics in Context* Curriculum

Graphing Equations is the tenth unit in the algebra strand. The map below shows the complete *Mathematics in Context* curriculum for grade 8/9. It shows where the unit fits in the algebra strand and in the overall picture.

A detailed description of the units, the strands, and the connections in the *Mathematics in Context* curriculum can be found in the *Teacher Resource and Implementation Guide*.

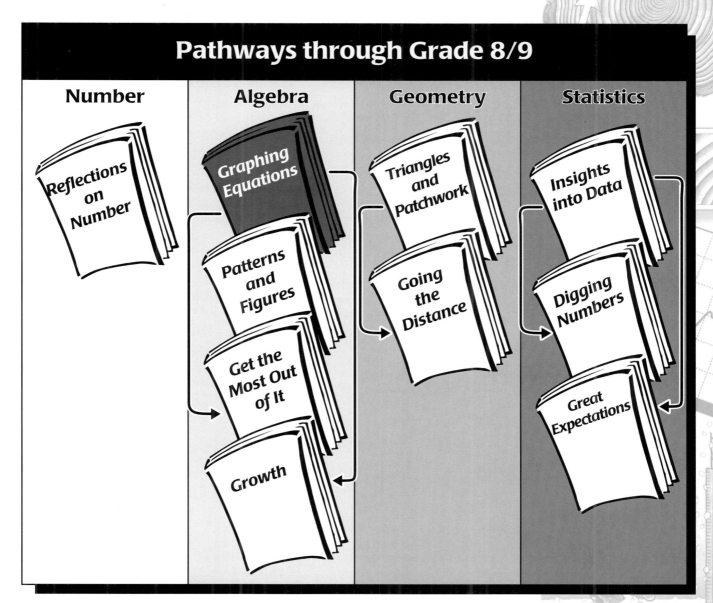

Pathways through Grade 8/9

Number

Reflections on Number

Algebra

Graphing Equations

Patterns and Figures

Get the Most Out of It

Growth

Geometry

Triangles and Patchwork

Going the Distance

Statistics

Insights into Data

Digging Numbers

Great Expectations

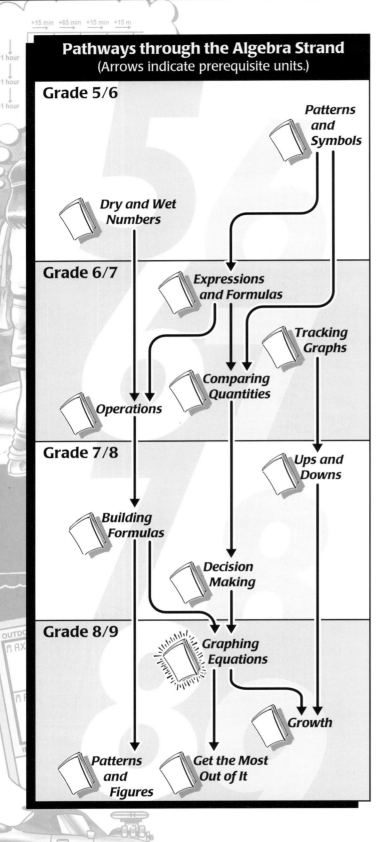

Pathways through the Algebra Strand
(Arrows indicate prerequisite units.)

Grade 5/6

Patterns and Symbols

Dry and Wet Numbers

Grade 6/7

Expressions and Formulas

Tracking Graphs

Comparing Quantities

Operations

Grade 7/8

Ups and Downs

Building Formulas

Decision Making

Grade 8/9

Graphing Equations

Growth

Patterns and Figures

Get the Most Out of It

Connections within the Algebra Strand

On the left is a map of the algebra strand; this unit, *Graphing Equations*, is highlighted.

Graphing Equations is the first unit of the algebra strand for grade 8/9. In this unit, many of the informal and pre-formal notions and concepts from previous algebra units are made formal. The unit is preceded by the grade 7/8 unit *Building Formulas*, in which students worked with formulas and expressions, and by the grade 6/7 unit *Tracking Graphs* and the grade 7/8 unit *Ups and Downs*, in which the emphasis is on graphing. In these units, students investigated lines in a variety of contexts. In the grade 8/9 unit *Growth*, nonlinear graphs are formalized.

Equations and the principle of fair exchange are introduced in the grade 6/7 unit *Comparing Quantities* and used in the grade 7/8 unit *Decision Making*. In *Graphing Equations,* these informal ideas about slope are further formalized.

Graphing Equations is a point in the algebra strand where all three substrands come together: expressions and formulas (mathematical notation of relationships), equations and inequalities (solving them and using them to describe situations), and graphs (using them to represent processes). In the units that follow *Graphing Equations*, students continue working with the equation and graph of a straight line, further formalizing the algebra that they learned in grades 5–7.

A variety of linear, quadratic, and exponential relationships will be investigated in a more formal way in the grade 8/9 unit *Growth*. The more formal uses of formulas will be further investigated in the grade 8/9 unit *Patterns and Figures*. The mathematics of solving systems of equations and linear programming is further formalized in the grade 8/9 unit *Get the Most Out of It*.

The Algebra Strand

Grade 5/6

Patterns and Symbols
Using symbols to represent patterns, creating equivalent patterns, and making generalizations from them to find a rule.

Dry and Wet Numbers
Developing the concept of negative numbers, adding with positive and negative numbers, interpreting a drawing using a scale, and making a scale line with positive and negative numbers.

Grade 6/7

Expressions and Formulas
Describing series of calculations using operation strings, generalizing to find a formula, and representing relationships found in tables.

Tracking Graphs
Producing line graphs, reading data from graphs, and learning to look at a graph's essential features rather than details.

Comparing Quantities
Organizing and translating information from stories using symbols, charts, tables, and equations.

Operations
Multiplying and dividing, adding and subtracting positive and negative numbers; and plotting ordered pairs in all four quadrants of the coordinate plane.

Grade 7/8

Building Formulas
Relating tables to algebraic descriptions, applying recursive and direct-rule formulas, relating expressions in equivalent forms, and using squares and square roots to solve area problems.

Ups and Downs
Describing an increasing or decreasing function from a table or graph, determining whether or not a growth function is linear, and recognizing a periodic function.

Decision Making
Representing data with graphs, working with the notion of constraints and with graphing inequalities, and graphing discrete functions.

Powers of Ten
Investigating simple laws for calculating with powers of 10 and investigating very large and very small numbers. (*Powers of Ten* is also in the number strand.)

Grade 8/9

Graphing Equations
Graphing points and lines in the coordinate plane; solving single-variable linear equations; using inequalities to describe restricted regions on a graph; and learning the structure of the equation of a line.

Patterns and Figures
Recognizing regularity in patterns; expressing generalities; exploring progressions, rectangular and triangular numbers, and Pascal's triangle.

Growth
Investigating linear, quadratic, cubic, and exponential functions; using recursive and direct formulas; and describing growth with graphs.

Get the Most Out of It
Solving word problems with two unknowns; solving systems of equations; graphing lines, inequalities, and hyperbolas; and working with curved feasible regions.

Connections with Other *Mathematics in Context* Units

Graphing Equations, a pivotal unit in the *Mathematics in Context* curriculum, deals with linear relationships. It has many connections with units in all other strands. Slope as the tangent of an angle is introduced in the geometry strand units *Figuring All the Angles, Looking at an Angle,* and *Going the Distance.* Graphs as representations of information play an important role in the statistics strand as well, where linear relationships are graphed. In the unit *Insights into Data,* linear regressions are further explored. *Graphing Equations* also makes connections with the number strand, concerning the use of the relationship between two numbers as expressed in a ratio.

The following mathematical topics that are included in the unit *Graphing Equations* are introduced or further developed in other *Mathematics in Context* units.

Prerequisite Topics

Topic	Unit	Grade
wind directions and angle measures	*Figuring All the Angles *	5/6
	*Made to Measure *	6/7
	*Looking at an Angle *	7/8
coordinate grids	*Operations*	6/7
slope	*Looking at an Angle *	7/8
parallel lines	*Triangles and Beyond *	7/8
the four quadrants positive and negative numbers	*Operations*	6/7
graphs	*Tracking Graphs*	6/7
	Ups and Downs	7/8
maps	*Figuring All the Angles *	5/6
	*Ways to Go **	7/8
regions	*Decision Making*	7/8
inequality signs	*Decision Making*	7/8
	Operations	6/7
fair exchange, slope	*Comparing Quantities*	6/7
	Decision Making	7/8
formulas	*Expressions and Formulas*	6/7

Topics Revisited in Other Units

Topic	Unit	Grade
coordinate grids	*Get the Most Out of It*	8/9
	Growth	8/9
fair exchange, slope	*Get the Most Out of It*	8/9
straight lines	*Get the Most Out of It*	8/9
	*Insight into Data **	8/9
	Patterns and Figures	8/9
maps, tangent, angles	*Going the Distance *	8/9

    * These units in the geometry strand also help students make connections to ideas about algebra.
   ** These units in the statistics strand also help students make connections to ideas about algebra.

Student Materials and Teaching Notes

Student Book
Table of Contents

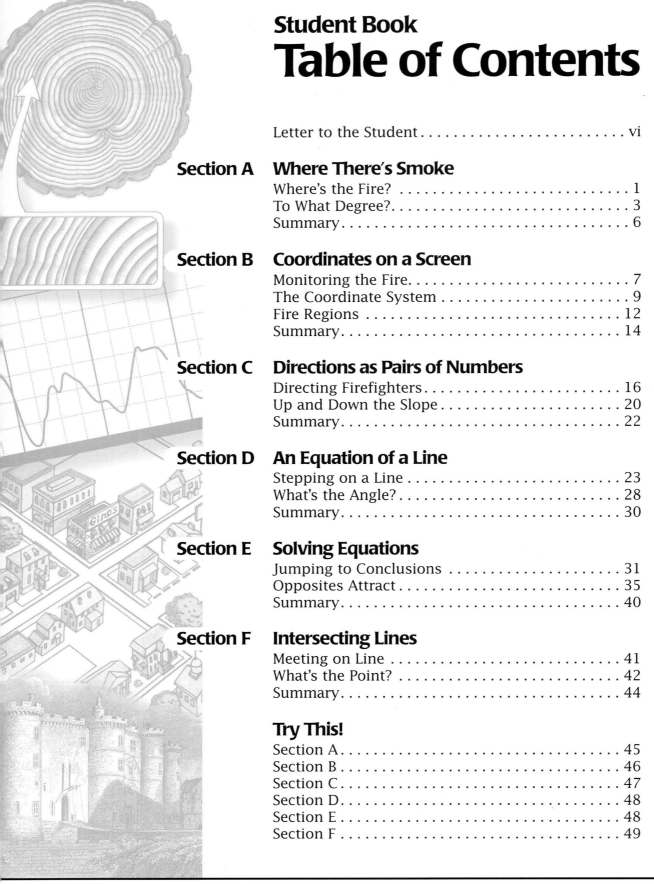

Dear Student,

You will soon begin the unit *Graphing Equations.* The focus of this unit is the study of lines. At first you will investigate how forest fires can be reported by park rangers at observation towers. You will learn many different ways to describe directions, lines, and locations. As you do, keep an eye out for other uses of lines and coordinates in your day-to-day activities.

As part of this unit, you will use a graphing calculator to explore several ways to find the point of intersection of two lines. After you complete this unit, you will be able to use a graphing calculator to discover many more features of lines, points, coordinates, and equations.

We hope you will enjoy this unit.

Sincerely,

The Mathematics in Context Development Team

Work Students Do

Students locate forest fires on a map using the eight "wind directions" from fixed positions (fire towers). Students locate the position of each fire by considering its direction from two different fire towers. Students then refine their location-finding system by using degree measurements.

Goals

Students will:

- describe and graph directions using wind directions and angles;
- understand how to find the intersection point of two lines graphically;
- model a problem situation and translate it to a graph or an equation.*

  * *This goal is introduced in this section and is assessed in other sections of the unit.*

Pacing

- approximately one to two 45-minute class sessions

Vocabulary

- compass rose
- degree measurements

About the Mathematics

Describing directions is an important concept in geometry. By giving directions, students learn, how to use symbols, how mathematics can relate to their lives, and the need for precision. Directions can be described in words, symbols (N, E, S, W), degrees, and with other measurements such as with coordinates relating to a coordinate grid system, or with slope. Students may remember directions and degrees from the grades 5/6 and 7/8 geometry units.

The way in which directions are given on a map is a matter of convention (much like the metric system or customary system of measurement). One way of giving directions is to divide a circle into wind directions. Wind directions are usually used to describe only the eight main directions. A more refined way of giving directions is to divide the circle even more, into 360 degrees. (Actually, even 360 degrees are sometimes not precise enough. Degrees can be subdivided still further into 60 minutes per degree and 60 seconds per minute.)

Locating fires from fixed positions (the fire towers) provides students with experiences that later in the unit lead to the definition of the slope of a line and the equation of a line.

Materials

- Letter to the Family, page 114 of the Teacher Guide (one per student)
- Student Activity Sheets 1–3, pages 115–117 of the Teacher Guide (one of each per student)
- rulers, pages 9 and 15 of the Teacher Guide (one per student)
- compass cards, pages 11, 13, 15, and 17 of the Teacher Guide (one per student)
- protractors, pages 13, 15, and 17 of the Teacher Guide, optional (one per student)

Planning Instruction

You may want to introduce this section by discussing magnetic compasses, and how they are used to navigate in remote locations such as forests. You might also bring in two or more compasses and have students try to identify objects in the classroom (or even in the whole school) given directions from two different locations in the room (or school).

Students may work on problems 1, 2 and 9 individually. Problems 7 and 8 may be done individually or in small groups. . The remaining problems may be done in small groups.

There are no optional problems in this section.

Homework

Problems 7 and 8 (page 14 of the Teacher Guide) may be assigned as homework. The Extension (page 13 of the Teacher Guide) and the Writing Opportunity (page 17 of the Teacher Guide) may also be assigned as homework. After students finish Section A, you may assign appropriate activities from the Try This! section located on pages 45–49 of the *Graphing Equations* Student Book. The Try This! activities reinforce the key mathematical concepts introduced in this section.

Planning Assessment

- Problem 4 can be used to informally assess students' ability to understand how to find the intersection point of two lines graphically.
- Problem 9 can be used to informally assess students' ability to describe and graph directions using wind directions and angles.

A. WHERE THERE'S SMOKE

Where's the Fire?

Forest rangers watch for smoke from tall fire towers. To fight a fire, firefighters need to know the exact location of the fire and whether it is spreading. Forest rangers watching fires are in constant telephone communication with the firefighters.

Overview Students are introduced to the context of locating forest fires from fire towers. This context will be used throughout the unit. There are no problems on the page for students to solve.

About the Mathematics In this section, directions are described using the eight main wind directions (north, northeast, south, southeast, and so on) and degree measurements, where 0 degrees is North and measurements progress clockwise. Students may remember this notation from the grade 5/6 unit *Figuring All the Angles* and from the grade 7/8 unit *Looking at an Angle.*

In mathematics, the convention is to place the positive *x*-axis (east) at zero degrees and to measure counterclockwise.

Extension You may want to have students look at a map of a park and try to locate fire towers. They can use this map throughout the unit to relate what they learn to another situation.

The map on the right shows two fire towers at points *A* and *B*. The eight-pointed star in the upper right corner of the map, called a "compass rose," shows eight directions: north, northeast, east, southeast, south, southwest, west, and northwest. The two towers are 10 kilometers apart and, as the compass rose indicates, they lie on a north-south line.

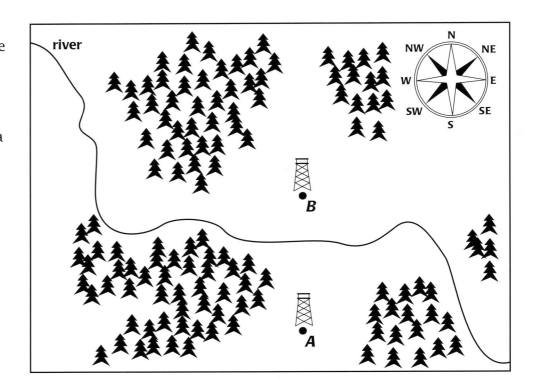

One day the rangers at both fire towers observe smoke in the forest.

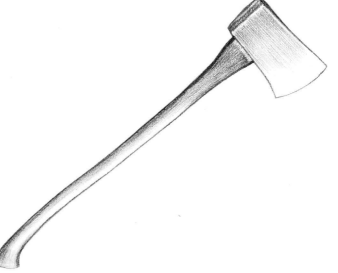

1. The rangers at tower *A* report that the smoke is directly northwest of their tower. Is this information enough to tell the firefighters the exact location of the fire? Explain why or why not.

2. The rangers at tower *B* report that the smoke is directly southwest of their tower. Use **Student Activity Sheet 1** to indicate the location of the fire.

1. No. There are many points on the straight line that lead northwest from tower *A*.

2. Students should draw lines from tower *A* to the northwest and from tower *B* to the southwest. The intersection point of the two lines is the location of the fire, as the map below shows.

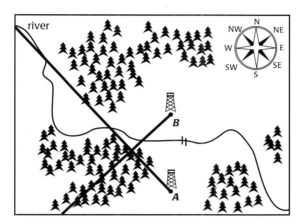

Materials Student Activity Sheet 1 (one per student); rulers (one per student)

Overview Students use a compass rose to locate a fire.

About the Mathematics The eight main directions shown on the compass rose can be further refined. In this unit, however, only the eight major wind directions are used.

Planning Students may work on problems **1** and **2** individually.

Comments about the Problems

1–2. Before students begin problem **1,** make sure that they understand how to read the map. Students should do these problems by drawing straight lines using a ruler and the directions indicated in the compass rose on the map. Students do not need to use a compass card.

   1. Students should realize that one direction from one point is not enough information to locate a second point; the second point could be anywhere on the ray that moves in that direction.

   2. When a direction from another point is introduced, the location of the fire can be determined.

To What Degree?

In problems **1** and **2,** you used the eight points of a compass rose to describe directions. You can also use degree measurements to describe directions.

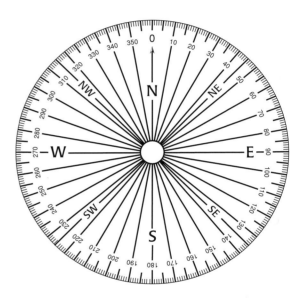

A complete circle contains 360°. North is typically aligned with 0° (or 360°). Continuing in a clockwise direction, notice that east corresponds with 90°, south with 180°, and west with 270°.

3. a. What degree measurement corresponds to the direction NE? What degree measurement corresponds to SE?

   b. What compass direction is opposite NE? What compass direction is opposite SE?

   c. What degree measurements correspond to the *opposites* of NE and SE?

4. Which system—compass directions or degree measurements—would you recommend for rangers to report fires? Why?

3. a. Northeast: 45°
Southeast: 135°

b. Opposite to northeast: southwest

Opposite to southeast: northwest

c. Southwest: 225°
Northwest: 315°

4. Answers will vary. Students may note that if rangers use the system with degree measurements, they can report the locations of the fires more accurately.

Materials compass cards (one per student)

Overview Students review how to use a compass card, which they may remember from the grade 5/6 unit *Figuring All the Angles* and the grade 7/8 unit *Looking at an Angle.* Students use the cards to measure directions.

Planning You may want to review how to use a compass card in a brief class discussion. Students may work on problems **3** and **4** in small groups. Problem **4** can be used as an informal assessment.

Comments about the Problems

3. Students may find the degree measurements of NE, SE, SW, and NW by starting with 45° and then using any of the following strategies:

- add multiples of 90° to 45°;
- find patterns in the numbers (45, 135, 225, and 315).

Students may know that in navigation, north is 0°, and headings are read clockwise relative to that.

4. Informal Assessment This problem assesses students' ability to understand how to find the intersection point of two lines.

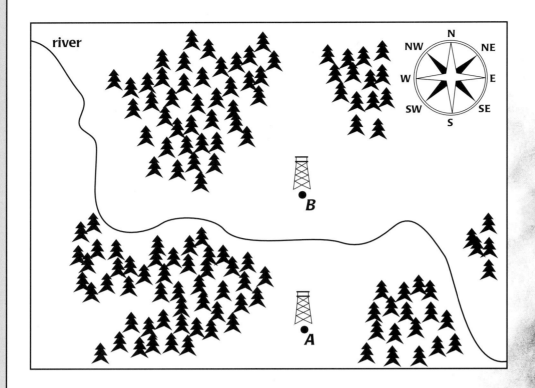

5. Smoke is reported at 8° from tower *A*, and the same smoke is reported at 26° from tower *B*. Use **Student Activity Sheet 2** to show the exact location of the fire.

6. Use **Student Activity Sheet 2** to show the exact location of a fire if rangers report smoke at 342° from tower *A* and 315° from tower *B*.

5.

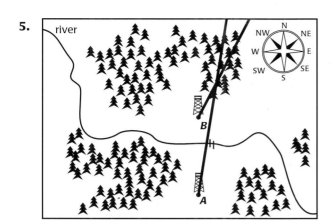

6.

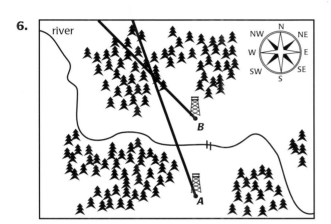

Materials Student Activity Sheet 2 (one per student); compass cards (one per student); protractors, optional (one per student)

Overview Students locate more fires in the park using a compass card.

Planning Students may work on problems **5** and **6** in small groups.

Comments about the Problems

5–6. By this time, all students should be able to use a compass card to draw lines when angles are given. You may also want to have protractors available for student use.

It is important that students try to measure as accurately as possible, but it is acceptable if there are small differences between their answers.

Students may have some interesting discussions when they use their own words to describe the locations of the fires.

Extension You may want to ask students to choose a location for the fire, and then find the angle at which the fire is seen from each tower.

There is a new tower at point *C.* It is 10 kilometers "due north" of tower *B,* as shown below. Use **Student Activity Sheet 3** for problems **7** and **8.**

7. The firefighters receive reports of smoke that is 294° from tower *A,* 247° from tower *B,* and 210° from tower *C.*

    a. The firefighters know that something is wrong with these reports. Explain how they know.

    b. Further reports confirm that the observations from towers *A* and *C* are correct but the observation from tower *B* is incorrect. Find the correct observation to report from tower *B.*

8. On another day, rangers report smoke at a direction of 240° from tower *A and* from tower *B.* Is it possible that both reports are correct? Why or why not?

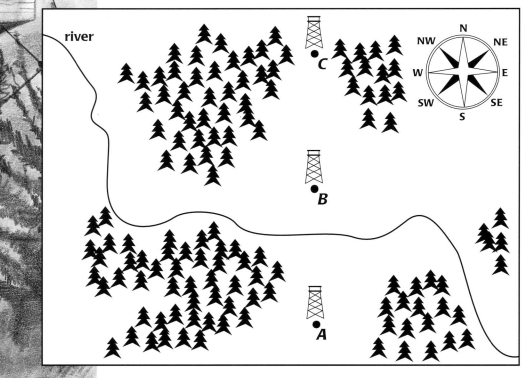

7. a. The three directions do not determine a single point, so at least one report must be wrong.

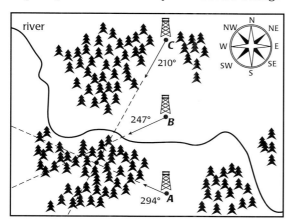

b. Tower *B*'s direction should have been about 238°. This direction can be determined by drawing a line from the intersection of the lines from tower *A* and tower *C* to tower *B*.

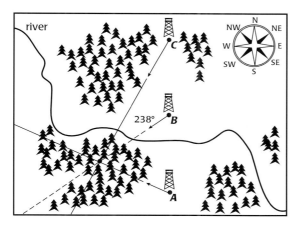

8. No, at least one report must be incorrect, because the lines going in the same direction are parallel. Parallel lines do not intersect.

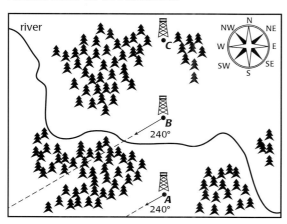

Materials Student Activity Sheet 3 (one per student); compass cards (one per student); rulers (one per student); protractors, optional (one per student)

Overview Students locate more fires using degree measurements. They discover that when the directions from two towers are the same, at least one report must be wrong.

About the Mathematics When directions are the same, the corresponding lines of vision are parallel. Parallel lines do not intersect, so it is impossible to locate a fire reported from a different location with the same direction. In the grade 7/8 unit *Triangles and Beyond,* students studied parallel lines in depth.

Planning Students may work on problems **7** and **8** individually or in small groups. These problems may also be assigned as homework.

Comments about the Problems

7–8. Homework These problems may be assigned as homework.

8. You might want to discuss the possibility that the fire is very far away.

Did You Know From a tower 30 meters high, you can see about 20 kilometers. In general, you can use the following rule:

If a tower is *h* meters tall, the distance you can see is 3.6 $\sqrt{h}$ kilometers.

Summary

You have seen two ways to indicate a direction from a point on a map.

- Using a compass rose, you can indicate one of the eight directions: N, NE, E, SE, S, SW, W, and NW.

- You can indicate direction using degree measurements; beginning with 0° for north, and measuring clockwise up to 360°.

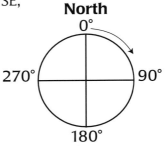

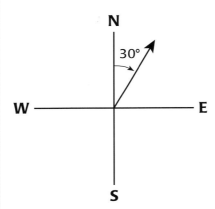

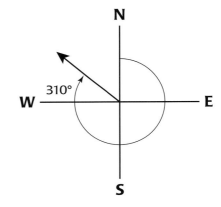

Summary Questions

9. a. The direction 30° is shown above on the left. What direction is opposite 30°?

   b. What direction is shown above on the right? What degree measurement is the opposite of that direction?

9. a. 210°

   b. 310°; 130°

Materials compass cards, optional (one per student); protractors, optional (one per student)

Overview Students read the Summary, which reviews the main concepts covered in this section.

Planning Students may work on problem **9** individually. This problem can also be used as an informal assessment. After students finish Section A, you may assign appropriate activities from the Try This! section, located on pages 45–49 of the *Graphing Equations* Student Book, for homework.

Comments about the Problems

9. Informal Assessment This problem assesses students' ability to describe directions using angles.

Students may use their compass cards or protractors to answer these questions.

Writing Opportunity You may want to ask students to use a map of their own to write some problems about directions. They should also give the answers to their own problems.

Work Students Do

In this section, students continue to locate fires on a map, but instead of using wind directions or degree measurements, they use a coordinate grid. Locations are given as (x, y) positions on the grid. Students explore how the (x, y) positions change as the fire moves in different directions. They use equations to describe the movement of fires along lines. Students draw firebreaks that follow parts of horizontal and vertical lines. Then they use inequalities to describe regions that are enclosed by firebreaks.

Goals

Students will:

- describe and graph directions using wind directions and angles;*

- understand and graph horizontal and vertical lines and their equations;

- use inequalities to describe regions restricted by horizontal and vertical lines;

- understand the graph of a line in the coordinate plane;

- model a problem situation and translate it to a graph or an equation.*

* These goals are assessed in other sections of the unit.

Pacing

- approximately two to three 45-minute class sessions

Vocabulary

- < and > signs
- coordinate system
- equation
- horizontal line
- origin
- quadrant
- vertical line
- x-axis
- x-coordinate
- y-axis
- y-coordinate

About the Mathematics

The purpose of this section is to review the coordinate grid system that was formally introduced in the grade 6/7 unit *Operations* and to make sure students understand movements on the coordinate system. Students have already learned to find locations on a map using degrees and wind directions. The (x, y) notation is another way of finding locations, but it differs from the first two types of notation in that it does not give a direction. Directions involving the coordinate grid will be introduced in the next section, as students are introduced to the concept of slope.

Vertical lines have equations of the form $x = a$ (for example, $x = 1$, $x = -2$, and so on). In a vertical line, the x-coordinate is fixed. A vertical line is the set of all points whose x-coordinate is the same. Horizontal lines have equations of the form $y = b$ (for example, $y = 1$, $y = -2$, and so on). In a horizontal line, the y-coordinate is fixed. A horizontal line is the set of all points whose y-coordinate is the same. Inequality signs have been introduced and used in the grade 6/7 unit *Operations* and the grade 7/8 unit *Decision Making*. In this unit, inequality signs are used to describe regions.

Materials

- Student Activity Sheet 4, page 118 of the Teacher Guide (one per student)
- local area or park maps, page 25 of the Teacher Guide, optional (one per student)
- compass cards, page 27 of the Teacher Guide (one per student)
- centimeter rulers, pages 31 and 33 of the Teacher Guide (one per student)
- transparency of Student Activity Sheet 4, pages 31 and 33 of the Teacher Guide, optional (one per class)
- overhead projector, pages 31 and 33 of the Teacher Guide, optional (one per class)
- graph paper, page 35 of the Teacher Guide, optional (one sheet per student)

Planning Instruction

You may want to introduce this section by discussing the importance of forest fires for maintaining ecological balance. Students might also have some experience with firebreaks in nearby forests. Many parks use volunteers to help with controlled burns (deliberately set fires that prevent serious damage from uncontrolled fires).

Students may do problems 7, 8, 15, and 16 individually or in small groups. Problems 11–13 and 17–19 may be done individually. The remaining problems may be done in small groups.

There are no optional problems in this section.

Homework

Problems 7 (page 26 of the Teacher Guide), 8 (page 28 of the Teacher Guide), and 15–16 (page 32 of the Teacher Guide) may be assigned as homework. The Extensions (pages 25 and 33 of the Teacher Guide) and the Writing Opportunity (page 35 of the Teacher Guide) may also be assigned as homework. After students finish Section B, you may assign appropriate activities from the Try This! section located on pages 45–49 of the *Graphing Equations* Student Book. The Try This! activities reinforce the key mathematical concepts introduced in this section.

Planning Assessment

- Problem 13 can be used to informally assess students' ability to understand and graph horizontal and vertical lines and their equations. This problem also assesses their ability to use inequalities to describe regions restricted by horizontal and vertical lines.

- Problems 17, 18, and 19 can be used to informally assess students' ability to understand and graph horizontal and vertical lines and their equations. These problems also assess their ability to understand the graph of a line in the coordinate plane.

B. COORDINATES ON A SCREEN

Monitoring the Fire

The park supervisor uses a computerized map of the
National Park to record and monitor activities in the park.

Solutions and Samples
of student work

Overview Students are introduced to the context of this section, computerized mapping of National Park activities. There are no problems on this page for students to solve.

About the Mathematics The advantage of a map with a grid over a map without a grid is that places on a grid map are easier to locate. A grid (or coordinate system) usually consists of two axes (a horizontal axis and a vertical axis), and scale marks that are at fixed intervals along the axes. The intersection of the two axes is called the origin.

Did You Know? In other sciences and disciplines, computer screens are also used to display maps of certain areas. Computerized mapping is used by airports for traffic control, by ships for radar, and by NASA to track objects that are orbiting or approaching Earth.

The computer screen below shows a map of the National Park. The shaded areas indicate woods. The plain areas indicate meadows and fields without trees. The numbers on the axes represent distances in kilometers.

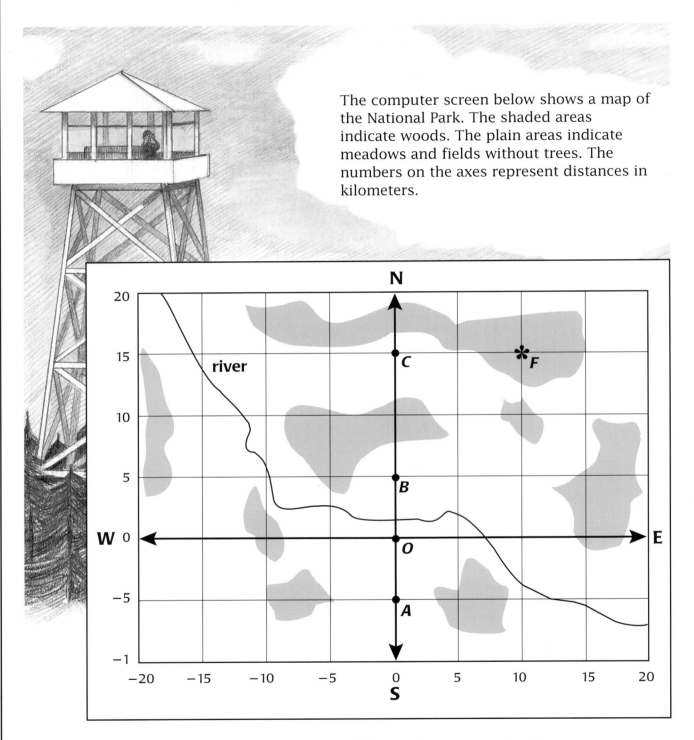

Point O on the screen represents the location of the park supervisor's office, and points A, B, and C are the rangers' towers.

1. a. What is the distance between towers A and B? Between tower C and point O?

 b. How is point O related to the positions of towers A and B?

1. **a.** The distance between towers *A* and *B* is 10 kilometers. The distance between tower *C* and point *O* is 15 kilometers.

   b. Point *O* is halfway between towers *A* and *B*.

Overview Students explore the computer screen map of the National Park.

About the Mathematics Coordinates and the coordinate grid system have been introduced and used in earlier *Mathematics in Context* units. The coordinate system with four quadrants was formally introduced in *Operations*. Students worked with graphs in *Tracking Graphs* and *Ups and Downs*. Students also worked with maps in *Figuring All the Angles* and *Ways to Go*.

Planning Students may work on problem **1** in small groups.

Comments about the Problems

1. Before students begin working on this problem, you may want to discuss the main features of the map. Have students locate point *O* and towers *A*, *B*, and *C*. Be sure to discuss the scale of the map. Notice that the map on this page is different from the map used in Section A. In Section A, the map represented a smaller part of the park than what is displayed on the computer screen here.

The Coordinate System

A fire is spotted 10 kilometers east of point C. The location of that point (labeled F) is given by the coordinates 10 and 15. The coordinates of a point can be called the horizontal coordinate and the vertical coordinate, or they can be called the *x-coordinate* and the *y-coordinate*.

$$F = (10, 15)$$

horizontal coordinate or *x*-coordinate   vertical coordinate or *y*-coordinate

Use the map on page 8 to answer problems **2** through **4**.

2. Find the point that is halfway between C and F. What are the coordinates of that point?

3. Write the coordinates of the points that are:

   a. 10 kilometers west of B;

   b. 15 kilometers east of A;

   c. 15 kilometers west of A.

4. The coordinates of fire tower B are (0, 5).

   a. What are the coordinates of the fire towers at C and at A?

   b. What are the coordinates of the office at O?

2. (5, 15)

3. a. (−10, 5)

    b. (15, −5)

    c. (−15, −5)

4. a. Tower *C*: (0, 15)
      Tower *A*: (0, −5)

    b. Office at *O*: (0, 0)

Materials local area or park maps (one per student)

Overview Students review the terms x-*coordinate* and y-*coordinate*. They find the coordinates of several locations on the map.

About the Mathematics Students probably are already comfortable with the coordinate grid system, which was introduced in earlier *Mathematics in Context* units.

Planning Students may work on problems **2–4** in small groups.

Comments about the Problems

    2–4. Students should use the map on page 8 of the Student Book to answer the questions.

    2. Since point *F* and tower *C* have the same *y*-coordinate, the point halfway between them also has a *y*-coordinate of 15.

    3. Students should know that horizontal directions correspond to east–west and that vertical directions correspond to north–south.

Extension You may want to have students draw a coordinate grid system on a map of their own, and find the coordinates of some points on the map. Encourage students to use natural points as the centers of their maps. These central points should have the coordinates (0, 0).

The rangers' map is an example of a *coordinate system.* *O* is called the *origin* of the coordinate system.

The horizontal line through *O* is called the *x-axis.*
The vertical line through *O* is called the *y-axis.*

The two axes divide the screen into four parts: a NE section, a NW section, a SW section, and a SE section. Point *O* is a corner of each section, and the sections are called *quadrants.*

5. The coordinates of a point are both negative. Which quadrant is it in?

Use the map on page 8 to answer problems **6** and **7**.

6. Find the point $(-20, -5)$ on the computer screen on page 8. What can you say about the position of this point in relation to point A?

7. There is a fire at point *F* (10, 15).

a. What directions, measured in degrees, should be given to the firefighters at towers *A, B,* and *C*?

b. A strong wind from the NE blows the fire to point *G,* which is 5 kilometers west and 5 kilometers south of *F.* What are the coordinates of *G*?

c. What instructions will fire towers *A, B,* and *C* send to the firefighters?

5. the southwest quadrant

6. The point is 20 kilometers west of tower *A*.

7. a. Tower *A*: 27°
Tower *B*: 45°
Tower *C*: 90°

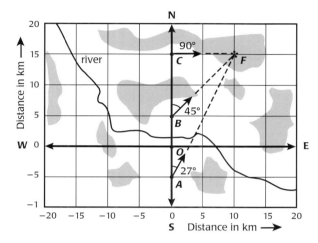

b. (5, 10)

c. Tower *A*: 18°
Tower *B*: 45°
Tower *C*: 135°

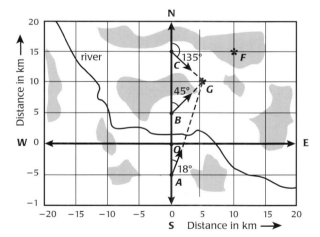

Materials compass cards (one per student)

Overview Students are introduced to the formal terms *coordinate system, origin, quadrants, x-axis,* and *y-axis*. These terms have also been introduced and used in earlier *Mathematics in Context* units. Students determine the locations of fires relative to each tower.

About the Mathematics Directions and coordinates are related to each other. On this page, this relationship is addressed informally. Later in the unit, students will learn how to relate angles to coordinates.

Planning Students may work on problems **5** and **6** in small groups. They may do problem **7** individually or in small groups. Problem **7** may also be assigned as homework.

Comments about the Problems

5–7. Before students begin working on these problems, you may want to review the terminology related to the coordinate system. You may want to refer to earlier *Mathematics in Context* units to remind students of the meanings of these terms and how to use them.

7. Homework This problem may be assigned as homework. You may want to remind students that when a wind blows *from* the northeast, it blows *to* the opposite direction, southwest.

The computer screen can be refined with horizontal and vertical lines that represent a grid of distances 1 kilometer apart so the side of each small square represents 1 kilometer.

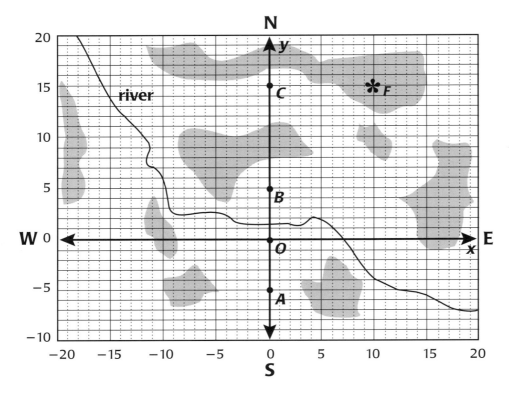

8. The screen above shows a river going from NW to SE.

   a. What are the coordinates of the two points where the river leaves the screen?

   b. What are the coordinates of the points where the river crosses the *x*-axis? Where does it cross the *y*-axis?

9. A fire is moving from north to south, and its position is moving along a vertical line on the screen.

   a. The fire started at (10, 15). What are its positions after it has moved 1 kilometer south? After it has moved 2 kilometers south? After 3 kilometers south? After 10 more kilometers south?

   b. Describe what happens to the *x*-coordinate of the moving fire.

10. A wind is spreading a fire so that its *y*-coordinate is not changing. Describe the direction of the wind.

8. a. The river leaves the screen at coordinates (−18, 20) and (20, −7).

   b. The river crosses the *x*-axis at (7, 0) and the *y*-axis at approximately (0, 1.5).

9. a. (10, 14) after 1 kilometer
   (10, 13) after 2 kilometers
   (10, 12) after 3 kilometers
   (10, 3) after 10 more kilometers

   b. The *x*-coordinate stays the same.

10. The wind is moving from the east or west.

Overview Students find the coordinates of the locations where a river leaves the screen and where it crosses the *x*- and *y*-axes. They investigate what happens to the coordinates of a fire when it moves horizontally and vertically.

About the Mathematics The place where the river crosses one of the axes of the graph is called the *x*-intercept (crossing the *x*-axis) or the *y*-intercept (crossing the *y*-axis). The term *y-intercept* will be introduced formally in Section D. When something moves vertically, the *x*-coordinate stays the same. When something moves horizontally, the *y*-coordinate stays the same.

Planning Students may work on problem **8** individually or in small groups. This problem may also be assigned as homework. Students may work on problems **9** and **10** in small groups.

Comments about the Problems

8. Homework This problem may be assigned as homework. The terms *horizontal* and *vertical* may help some students and hinder others. If students have difficulty remembering the difference between the two words, you might remind them that the horizon is horizontal.

   b. The answer given in the solutions column for the point at which the river crosses the *y*-axis is approximate. Accept answers that are reasonably close to the given answer.

9. a. Make sure students understand that the fire is moving continuously along the entire line of points with *x*-coordinates that are equal to 10.

Vertical and horizontal lines have special descriptions. For example, a *vertical line* that is 10 kilometers east of the origin can be described by $x = 10$.

11. a. Why does $x = 10$ describe a vertical line 10 kilometers east of the origin?

    b. How would you describe a *horizontal line* that is 5 kilometers north of point O? Explain your answer.

12. a. Where on the screen is the line described by $x = -5$?

    b. Where on the screen is the line described by $y = 15$?

> The description $x = 10$ is called an *equation* of the vertical line that is 10 kilometers east of O. Also, $y = 10$ is called an equation of the horizontal line that is 10 kilometers north of O.

Fire Regions

To prevent forest fires from spreading, parks and forests usually contain a network of wide strips of land that have only low grasses or clover called firebreaks. These firebreaks are maintained by mowing or grazing.

13. There are firebreaks that follow parts of the lines described by the equations $x = 14$, $x = 16$, $x = 18$, $y = 8$, $y = 6$, $y = 4$, $y = 2$, and $y = 0$.

    a. Using **Student Activity Sheet 4,** draw the firebreaks through the wooded regions of the park.

    b. Which of these firebreaks is the longest? Approximately how long is it?

11. a. Answers will vary. Some students may say that $x = 10$ is a vertical line that crosses the x-axis at 10. Another answer would be that every point on the line has an x-coordinate of 10 which means that the x-coordinate is fixed.

  b. $y = 5$. Explanations will vary. Sample explanation:

  All points on this horizontal line have a y-coordinate of 5.

12. a. The line $x = -5$ is a vertical line crossing the x-axis 5 kilometers west of the y-axis.

  b. The line $y = 15$ is a horizontal line crossing the y-axis 15 kilometers north of the x-axis.

13. a.

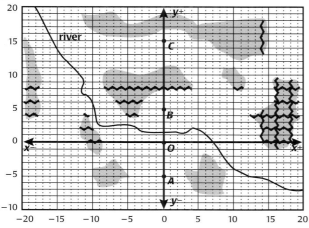

  b. The longest fire break is located on the line $y = 8$ and is approximately 11 kilometers long.

Materials Student Activity Sheet 4 (one per student); centimeter rulers (one per student); transparency of Student Activity Sheet 4, optional (one per class); overhead projector, optional (one per class)

Overview Students use equations to describe horizontal and vertical lines.

About the Mathematics At this point, the equations for horizontal and vertical lines are introduced. Later in this unit, the equations for other lines will be introduced.

Planning Students may work on problems **11–13** individually. Problem **13** can also be used as an informal assessment. Students should refer to the map on Student Book page 11 to answer problems **11** and **12**.

Comments about the Problems

11. Problem **11** is critical because this is where the equations of horizontal and vertical lines are introduced. For part **a,** students may answer, "because it crosses the x-axis at $x = 10$," which shows some understanding. There is no need to teach a more formal understanding of this concept at this time.

13. Informal Assessment This problem assesses students' ability to understand and graph horizontal and vertical lines and their equations. It also assesses their ability to use inequalities to describe regions restricted by horizontal and vertical lines.

  a. If students have difficulties, you might make a transparency of the map on Student Activity 4 in order to point out the regions through which the firebreaks will go.

  b. Be sure to tell students that this question refers to all of the firebreaks.

A fire is restricted by the four firebreaks that surround it. If a fire starts at the point (17, 5), the vertical firebreaks at $x = 16$ and $x = 18$ and the horizontal firebreaks at $y = 4$ and $y = 6$ will keep fire from spreading. Here is one way to describe the region:

x is between 16 and 18, y is between 4 and 6.

You can use inequalities to describe the region:

$16 < x < 18$ and $4 < y < 6$

(This is read "x is greater than 16 and less than 18, and y is greater than 4 and less than 6.")

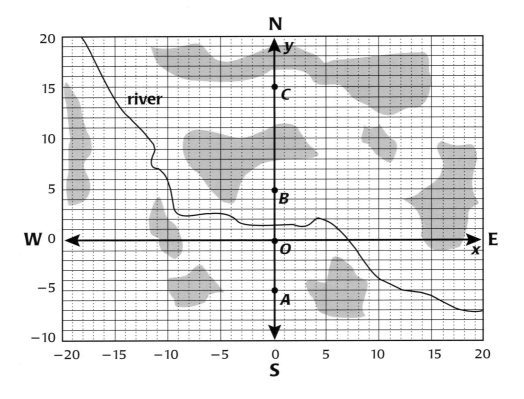

Use **Student Activity Sheet 4** for problems **14** through **16.**

14. Show the restricted region for a fire that starts at the point (17, 5).

15. Another fire starts at the point (15, 3). The fire is restricted to a region by four firebreaks. Show the region and describe it.

16. Use a pencil of a different color to show the region described by the inequalities $-6 < x < -3$ and $6 < y < 10$.

14.

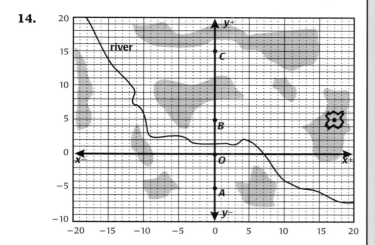

15. The region is $14 < x < 16$ and $2 < y < 4$.

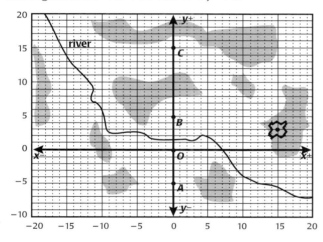

16.

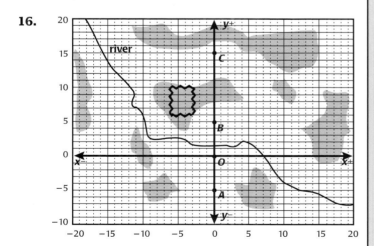

Materials Student Activity Sheet 4 (one per student); centimeter rulers (one per student); transparency of Student Activity Sheet 4, optional (one per class); overhead projector, optional (one per class)

Overview Students review the use of inequalities to describe a region.

About the Mathematics Students were introduced to inequality signs in the grade 6/7 unit *Operations.* In the grade 7/8 unit *Decision Making*, students used inequality signs to describe regions.

Planning Students may work on problem **14** in small groups. They may work on problems **15** and **16** individually or in small groups. Problems **15** and **16** can also be assigned as homework.

Comments about the Problems

14–16. Before students begin working on these problems, you may want to discuss the inequality signs and how to use them. Students may remember how to use inequality signs from the grade 7/8 unit *Decision Making.*

You may want to make a transparency of Student Activity Sheet 4 so that students can show the restricted regions of the fires on the overhead projector. You may also want to remind students that there are firebreaks only in wooded areas.

15–16. Homework These problems may be assigned as homework.

Extension You may want to have students make and describe regions on their own maps. Students can use the same maps that they used for the previous Extension activity in this section.

Summary

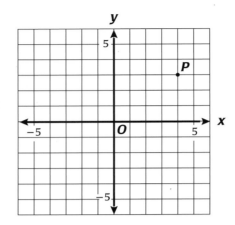

- In a coordinate system, the horizontal axis is called the *x*-axis and the vertical axis is called the *y*-axis. The axes intersect at the point (0, 0), called the origin.

- The location of a point is given by *x*- and *y*-coordinates (*x*, *y*).

- When points are on a vertical line, the *x*-coordinate does not change. Vertical lines can be described by equations such as $x = 1$, $x = 8$, and $x = -3$.

- When points are on a horizontal line, the *y*-coordinate does not change. Horizontal lines can be described by equations such as $y = -5$, $y = 0$, and $y = 3$.

- Inequalities can be used to describe a region. For example, $1 < x < 3$ and $-2 < y < 3$ describes a 2 by 5 rectangular region.

Summary Questions

17. What are the coordinates of *P* in the coordinate system above?

18. Suppose *P* moves on a straight line in a horizontal direction. What is an equation for that line?

19. In the coordinate system above, point *O* is the center of a rectangular region and *P* is one corner. The boundaries of the region are horizontal and vertical lines. Use inequalities to describe the region.

17. (4, 3)

18. $y = 3$

19. The following lines are the boundaries of the region:

$y = -3$ and $y = 3$, so $-3 < y < 3$
$x = -4$ and $x = 4$, so $-4 < x < 4$

Materials graph paper, optional (one sheet per student)

Overview Students read the Summary, which reviews the main concepts covered in this section. They also solve problems in which they find the coordinates of a given point and write the equations of horizontal and vertical lines.

About the Mathematics At the end of this section, students should understand equations for horizontal and vertical lines.

Planning Students may work on problems **17–19** individually. These problems can also be used as informal assessments. After students finish Section B, you may assign appropriate activities from the Try This! section, located on pages 45–49 of the *Graphing Equations* Student Book, for homework.

Comments about the Problems

17–19. Informal Assessment These problems assess students' ability to understand and graph horizontal and vertical lines and their equations. These problems also assess their ability to understand the graph of a line in the coordinate plane.

Writing Opportunity You may want to have students draw a coordinate system on a sheet of graph paper. Then, have them outline some regions and describe them using inequalities. Ask students to write a paragraph or two in their notebooks to explain all the features of the graph.

Work Students Do

In the previous section, students located fires on a coordinate grid map using (x, y) notation. The fires were all located relative to the origin, $(0, 0)$. In this section, students describe the location of a fire by using a horizontal and a vertical component. Students start by giving directions using pairs of numbers. They then learn to describe the slopes of lines using a single number, the ratio of the vertical component to the horizontal component.

Goals

Students will:

- understand the meaning of slope in different contexts;
- understand how to find the intersection point of two lines, graphically;*
- understand the graph of a line in the coordinate plane;
- model a problem situation and translate it to a graph or an equation.*

  These goals are assessed in other sections of the unit.

Pacing

- approximately two to three 45-minute class sessions

Vocabulary

- horizontal component
- slope
- vertical component

About the Mathematics

In previous sections of this unit, directions were given using wind directions, angle measures, and (x, y) notation. In this section, slopes of straight lines are related to directions. First, number pairs (see Teacher Guide page 40) and then the ratios of the number pairs (see Teacher Guide page 48) or slope are used to describe directions.

The slope of a line is a measure of how steep it is. It is given as the ratio of two numbers, the vertical change over the horizontal change. A line's slope is the same regardless of what two points on the line are used to compute it. A line with a positive slope moves up and to the right, while a line with a negative slope moves down and to the right.

Students informally studied slope in the grade 6/7 unit *Comparing Quantities* and in the grade 7/8 units *Decision Making* and *Looking at an Angle,* although in different contexts.

SECTION C. DIRECTIONS AS PAIRS OF NUMBERS

Materials

- Student Activity Sheets 5 and 6, pages 119 and 120 of the Teacher Guide (one of each per student)
- rulers, pages 47, 49, and 51 of the Teacher Guide (one per student)
- graph paper, page 51 of the Teacher Guide, optional (one sheet per student)

Planning Instruction

You may want to begin this section by reminding students that they have learned to describe specific points and regions using coordinate points and equations. Ask students, *When would you need to describe a line?* [Answers may vary. Students are about to learn that lines are useful in giving directions.]

Students may work on problems 1–7 in small groups. The remaining problems may be done individually.

Problem 19 is optional. If time is a concern, you may omit this problem or assign it as homework.

Homework

Problems 10 and 11 (page 44 of the Teacher Guide) may be assigned as homework. The Extensions (pages 43, 47, and 51 of the Teacher Guide) may also be assigned as homework. After students finish Section C, you may assign appropriate activities from the Try This! section, located on pages 45–49 of the *Graphing Equations* Student Book. The Try This! activities reinforce the key mathematical concepts introduced in this section.

Planning Assessment

- Problem 12 can be used to informally assess students' ability to understand the meaning of slope in different contexts.
- Problems 17–21 can be used to informally assess students' ability to understand the meaning of slope in different contexts and their ability to understand the graph of a line in the coordinate plane.

C. DIRECTIONS AS PAIRS OF NUMBERS

In the previous sections, directions from a point were indicated by compass references, such as N or NW. A second way to indicate directions involved using degrees measured clockwise from north, such as 30° or 210°. This section introduces a third method to indicate directions.

Overview Students are introduced to a third method of giving directions. There are no problems on this page for students to solve.

About the Mathematics In the previous section, students were introduced to coordinates. If the point from which you are looking is the origin of a coordinate system, the coordinates of a point indicate the direction in which you should look.

Planning You may want to introduce this section by reviewing how to indicate directions by using wind directions and degree measurements.

DIRECTING FIREFIGHTERS

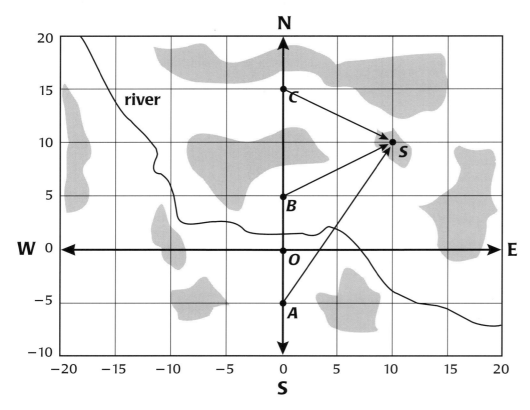

Smoke is reported at point S (10, 10). There is a fire fighting crew at tower B, so the crew needs to go 10 kilometers east and 5 kilometers north. Those instructions can be sent as the direction pair [+10, +5]. The first number gives the horizontal component of the direction, and the second number gives the vertical component.

1. a. Write a direction pair to describe the direction of the fire at point S as seen from point A.

   b. Do the same to describe point S as seen from point C. (*Hint:* You have to use a negative number.)

2. Using the top half of **Student Activity Sheet 5,** locate and label point G at (20, 15). Then use direction pairs to describe the location of G as seen from points A, B, and C.

Notice that for the rangers at tower B, the direction to point S is the same as the direction to point G. So we can say that the direction pairs [+10, +5] and [+20, +10] indicate the same direction from point B.

3. Why are they the same?

4. Find three different points on the map that are in the same direction from tower A.

1. a. [+10, +15]

  b. [+10, −5]

2. From point *A*: [+20, +20]

  From point *B*: [+20, +10]

  From point *C*: [+20, 0]

3. Answers will vary. Some students may say that all three points lie on the same straight line. Other students may indicate that the direction from point *B* to points *S* and *G* is 63°.

4. Answers will vary. One possible set of three points is as follows: (5, 0), (10, 5), and (15, 10). The common direction of these points from point *A* is given by [+5, +5], [+10, +10], or [+15, +15].

Materials Student Activity Sheet 5 (one per student)

Overview Students use direction pairs to describe directions and discover that the same direction can be given by more than one direction pair.

About the Mathematics A direction pair that describes the direction to a point in the coordinate system as looked at from the origin can be the same as the coordinates of that point. However, the coordinates that give the exact location of the point need not be the same as the direction pair. Any direction pair that describes the direction is fine. For example, the direction pair [2, 3] describes the same direction as [4, 6], and there are many points in this direction. Direction pairs can be used to describe directions from any point, not just from the origin.

Planning Before students begin to work on problems **1–4,** you may want to discuss the map on this page. Note that brackets ([ ]) are used to denote direction. Students may work on problems **1–4** in small groups.

Comments about the Problems

  1. If students have difficulty, you might have them describe this direction using compass directions first. For example, from point *A* the fire can be seen at 10 kilometers east and 15 kilometers north.

  3. Some students may notice that the ratio of the horizontal component of the direction pair to the vertical component is important. Any combination of numbers with the same ratio describes the same direction.

5. In the wooded area north of tower *B,* there is a fire. Name three points that are possible locations of that fire.

6. a. Give two direction pairs that indicate the direction NW.

   b. Give two direction pairs that indicate the direction SE.

7. What compass direction is indicated by [+1, 0]? What compass direction is indicated by [0, −1]?

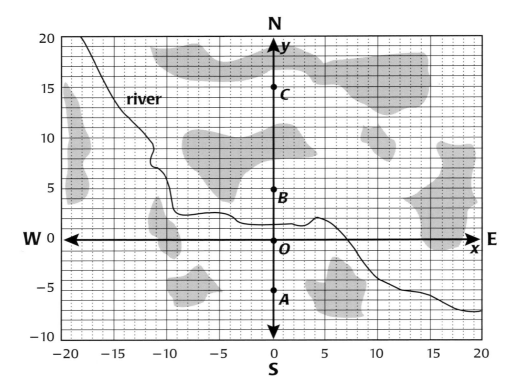

5. Answers will vary. Sample responses:

(0, 9), (0, 10), (0, 17)

6. a. Answers will vary. Sample response:

[−5, +5], [−10, +10]

Students' pairs should have a negative first number, and a positive second number. The ratio of the two numbers should be equal to −1.

b. Answers will vary. Sample response:

[+5, −5], [+10, −10]

Students' pairs should have a positive first number and a negative second number. The ratio of the two numbers should be equal to −1.

7. [+1, 0] = east

[0, −1] = south

Overview Students use direction pairs to describe directions. They also relate the directions described by direction pairs to the wind (or compass) directions that were used in Sections A and B.

About the Mathematics There are many direction pairs that can describe the same direction. Mathematicians often prefer to simplify the direction pair. Students do not need to do this simplifying, but they may appreciate the mathematician's preference.

Planning Students may work on problems **5–7** in small groups. When they are finished, you may want to have a short discussion about these problems to make sure all students understand the idea of direction pairs.

Comments about the Problems

6. This is the first time that the starting location for the direction pair is not given. Some students may naturally start at zero, but others might see that these direction pairs describe the correct wind direction from any starting location. This will be made more explicit later in this section. Students should recognize that these two directions are opposite. If students have difficulty seeing this, you might have them compare the direction pairs. The horizontal component and the vertical component in the solution to problem **6b** are the opposite of those in the solution to problem **6a.**

7. North and south are vertical directions. You might also ask students to describe the directions east and west using direction pairs.

Extension You may want to have students describe the eight main directions of the compass card with direction pairs, and then ask them to describe the patterns they see.

Use the graph on the top half of **Student Activity Sheet 5** for problems **8** through **10.**

8. Locate the fire based on the following reports:
   - Rangers at tower *B* observe smoke in the direction $[-9, +2]$.
   - Rangers at tower *C* observe smoke in the direction $[-3, -1]$.

9. Do the direction pairs $[-6, +9]$ and $[-8, +12]$ indicate the same direction? Use diagrams as part of your answer.

10. **a.** Locate and label four points that are in the direction $[+1, +1.5]$ from point *A.*

   b. What is a quick way to draw all the points that are in the direction $[+1, +1.5]$ from *A*?

11. For each two direction pairs below, explain why they indicate the same direction or different directions.

   a. $[+1, +3]$ and $[+4, +12]$

   b. $[+4, +3]$ and $[+8, -6]$

   c. $[-4, +3]$ and $[+8, -6]$

   d. $[+5, +8]$ and $[+6, +9]$

   e. $[+5, +8]$ and $[+1, +1.6]$

   f. $[+13, 0]$ and $[+25, 0]$

12. You can use many direction pairs to indicate a particular direction.

   a. Give five different direction pairs that indicate the direction $[+12, +15]$.

   b. What do all your answers to part **a** have in common?

8. The fire is located at the intersection point (−18, 9) of the two lines on the following map.

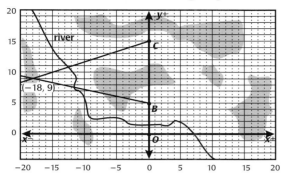

9. Yes, they do indicate the same direction. Some students may verify their answers by connecting points with a line drawn from the origin in this direction, as shown on the following graph:

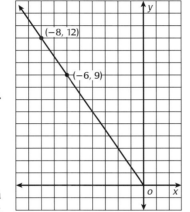

10. a. Answers will vary. Sample response: (2, −2), (4, 1), (6, 4), and (8, 7).

   b. Connect point *A* with one of the points in problem **10a** and extend it.

11. a. Same direction. Going right 1 and up 3 is the same direction as going right 4 and up 12.

   b. Different direction. The first pair moves right and up, and the second pair moves right and down.

   c. Different direction. The first pair goes to the left and second pair goes to the right.

   d. Different direction. The direction of the first pair [+5, +8] is along a line that would be slightly steeper than the direction of the second pair.

   e. Same direction. They both go right and up.

   f. Same direction. They both go due east.

12. a. Answers will vary. Sample response:

   [+4, +5], [+8, +10], [+24, +30], and [+16, +20]

   b. Answers may vary. Sample response:

   The ratio of the first number to the second (4:5) is the same in each answer.

Materials Student Activity Sheet 5 (one per student); graph paper (one per student)

Overview Students solve a series of problems in which directions are described with direction pairs.

About the Mathematics On this page, the concept of slope is informally explored. Directions are the same when the ratios of the numbers in the direction pairs are the same and the signs of the components match.

Planning Students may work on problems **8–12** individually. Problems **10** and **11** can also be assigned as homework. Problem **12** can be used as an informal assessment.

Comments about the Problems

   8. Unless students are careful, they will not locate the fire accurately. If students' answers are inaccurate, ask for justification.

   9–11. As students work on these problems, they should be developing the idea that the ratio of the numbers in each number pair is what is important for determining a unique direction.

   9. The graph in the solutions column shows the direction from the origin. Any other point on the line would also indicate the same direction.

   10–11. Homework These problems may be assigned as homework.

   11. Some students may select a point (like the origin) from which to begin. Others may just use the ratios of the numbers or the steepness of the steps to compare the directions. Some students might also make a connection to the idea of fair exchange discussed in the grade 6/7 unit *Comparing Quantities* or the grade 7/8 unit *Decision Making.* Students might also use a ratio table to generate more direction pairs.

   12. Informal Assessment This problem assesses students' ability to understand the meaning of slope in different contexts.

13. Use the map on the bottom of **Student Activity Sheet 5.**

   a. Label the point A $(0, -5)$ on the map.

   b. Show all the points on the map that are in the direction $[-1, +2]$ from A.

   c. Show all the points on the map that are in the direction $[+1, -2]$ from A.

   d. What do you notice in your answers for parts **b** and **c**?

The two number pairs $[+6, +4]$ and $[-9, -6]$ represent opposite directions. Below, all the points from B in the directions $[+6, +4]$ and $[-9, -6]$ are drawn. The result is a complete line.

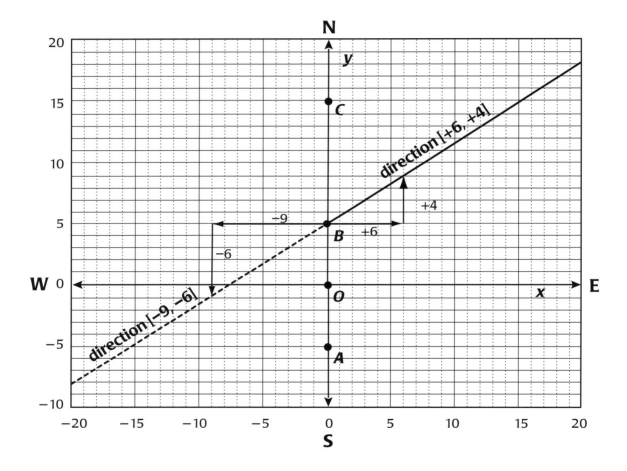

14. a. Give three other direction pairs on the solid part of the line through B.

   b. Give three other direction pairs on the dotted part of the line through B.

   c. What do all six direction pairs have in common?

13. a–c.

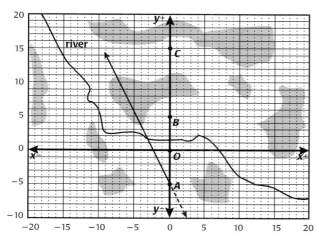

d. They form a complete line.

14. a. Answers will vary. Sample response:

[+3, +2], [+12, +8], [+9, +6]

b. Answers will vary. Sample response:

[−3, −2], [−12, −8], [−6, −4]

c. The ratio of the numbers (3:2) is the same in each direction pair.

Materials Student Activity Sheet 5 (one per student); rulers (one per student)

Overview Students investigate direction pairs that are opposites. They discover that direction pairs that are opposites form one line.

About the Mathematics A direction is always given from a point. A direction can be described with a direction pair. There are many different direction pairs that can describe a direction. To describe the same direction, the ratios of the numbers in the direction pairs must be the same, and the sign (positive, negative) of the ratio must be the same. The ratios of direction pairs that describe opposite directions are the same. The two line segments in one direction and the opposite direction together form a complete line.

Planning Students may work on problems **13** and **14** individually.

Comments about the Problems

13. All points that lie in the same direction and its opposite direction are on one line.

Extension You may want to have students return to the problems on previous pages and look for directions and opposite directions, to see what these number pairs have in common.

Up and Down the Slope

All the number pairs for a single direction and for the opposite of that direction have something in common: they all have the same ratio.

You can calculate two different ratios for a number pair:

horizontal component ÷ vertical component

or

vertical component ÷ horizontal component

Mathematicians frequently use the ratio

$$\frac{\text{vertical component}}{\text{horizontal component}}$$

and call that ratio the *slope* of a line.

$$\textbf{slope} = \frac{\textbf{vertical component}}{\textbf{horizontal component}}$$

15. Find the slope of the line joining all the points you drew in problem **13.**

Use **Student Activity Sheet 6** for problems **16** through **18.**

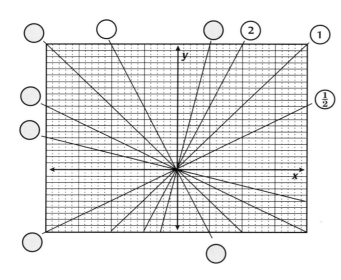

16. Each of the lines on the left contains the point (0, 0). For some of the lines, the slope is labeled inside its circle. Fill in the empty circles with the correct slope.

17. What do you know about two lines that contain the same slope?

18. Draw and label the line through (0, 0) whose slope is:

    a. $\frac{4}{3}$

    b. $-\frac{1}{2}$

15. The slope is -2. This ratio can be found by using either of the two directions:

- $[1, -2] = \frac{-2}{1} = -2$
- $[-1, 2] = \frac{2}{-1} = -2$

16.

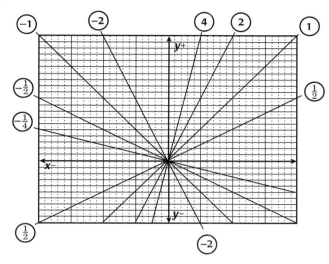

17. They form one complete line.

18. a–b.

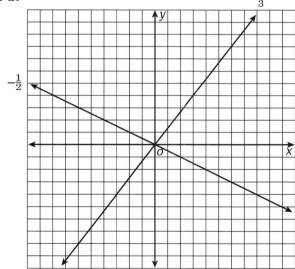

Materials Student Activity Sheet 6 (one per student); rulers (one per student)

Overview Students are introduced to slope as a measure to describe the direction or steepness of a line.

About the Mathematics In the grade 6/7 unit *Comparing Quantities* and the grade 7/8 unit *Decision Making,* students worked with the concept of fair exchange. The principle of fair exchange also leads to the concept of slope. In the grade 7/8 unit *Looking at an Angle,* the concept of slope is dealt with in a geometrical context, as the tangent of the angle that a line makes with the horizon. Slope is always the ratio of the vertical component to the horizontal component.

Planning Before students begin working on problems **15–18,** you may want to discuss the concept of slope. Remind students of previous units in which they have seen and worked with slope. Students may work on problems **15–18** individually. Problems **17** and **18** can be used as informal assessments.

Comments about the Problems

15. If students have difficulty, you might remind them to divide the vertical component by the horizontal component, not the other way around.

17–18. Informal Assessment These problems assess students' ability to understand the meaning of slope in different contexts and their ability to understand the graph of a line in the coordinate plane.

19. In the graph below, the two lines are not parallel.

   a. Find the slope of each line.

   b. This grid is too small to show the point where the two lines meet. Find the coordinates of this point, and explain your method for finding it.

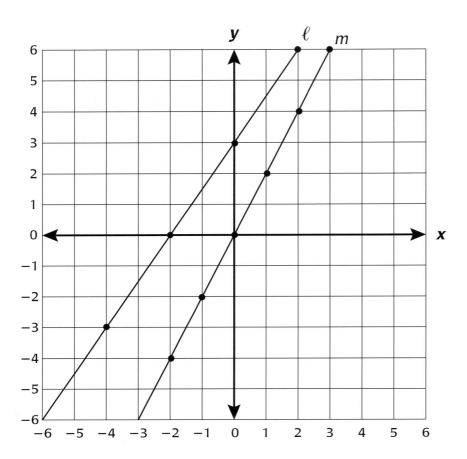

Solutions and Samples
of student work

19. a. The line (*m*) passing through the origin has a slope of 2. The line on the left has a slope of $\frac{3}{2}$.

b. The coordinates are (6, 12). Students may use a variety of strategies to solve this problem. Sample strategies:

Strategy 1

Some students may reason using the patterns in the vertical and horizontal distances between the two lines.

At $x = -2$, the vertical distance between the lines is 4.
At $x = 0$, the vertical distance between the lines is 3.
At $x = 2$, the vertical distance between the lines is 2.
At $x = 4$, the vertical distance between the lines is 1.
At $x = 6$, the vertical distance between the lines is 0.

At $y = 0$, the horizontal distance between the lines is 2.
At $y = 6$, the horizontal distance between the lines is 1.
At $y = 12$, the horizontal distance between the lines is 0.
So, at (6, 12) the distance is 0 for both *x* and *y*.

Strategy 2

Some students may redraw the two lines on a sheet of graph paper, extend the lines, find the place where they meet, and estimate the intersection point.

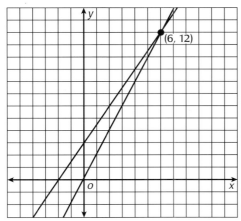

Materials rulers (one per student); graph paper, optional (one sheet per student)

Overview Students find the slopes of two lines and the point of intersection of these two lines.

About the Mathematics The slope of a line may be found by drawing any convenient right triangle using the line as the hypotenuse and then finding the ratio of the vertical component to the horizontal component.

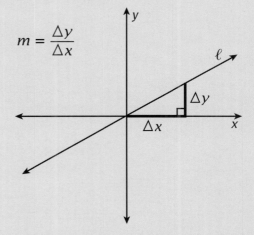

$$m = \frac{\Delta y}{\Delta x}$$

Planning Students may work on problem **19** individually. This problem is optional. If time is a concern, you may omit this problem or assign it as homework.

Comments about the Problems

19. Informal Assessment This problem assesses students' ability to understand the meaning of slope in different contexts and to understand the graph of a line in the coordinate plane.

As students work on this problem, you may want to have them discuss the connection between slope and parallel lines.

b. Students are not expected to solve a system of equations to find the point of intersection of these two lines. Encourage them to use an intuitive, informal strategy.

Extension You may want to provide students with more lines and ask them to find the slopes of the lines.

Summary

- You can indicate a direction from a point using a direction pair such as [+3, +2] or [+1, −1]. The first number is the horizontal component, and the second number is the vertical component.

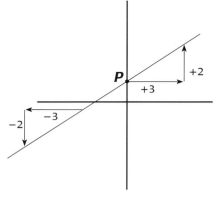 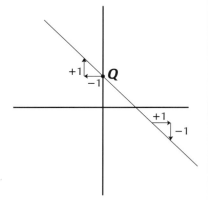

The points in the directions [+3, +2] and [−3, −2] are on the same line.

The points in the directions [+1, −1] and [−1, +1] are on the same line.

- All direction pairs in the same and opposite direction have the same ratio.

- The slope of a line is given by the ratio

$$\frac{\textbf{vertical component}}{\textbf{horizontal component}}$$

The slope of the line above on the left is $\frac{2}{3}$.
The slope of the line above on the right is −1.

Summary Questions

20. How many lines contain the two points (1, 2) and (26, 52)?

21. Find the slope of the line(s) in problem **20.**

20. There is only one line that contains these two points.

21. The slope is equal to 2.

Overview Students read the Summary, which reviews the main concepts covered in this section.

About the Mathematics The slope gives information about the direction of a line. A negative slope means that the line goes down; from upper left to lower right. A positive slope means that the line goes up; from lower left to upper right.

A line with a slope of 1 makes an angle of 45° with the positive x-axis. Lines with slopes that are smaller than 1 have angles between 0° and 45°. Lines with slopes larger than 1 make an angle between 45° and 90°. A vertical line has no slope, (the slope is undefined) since the horizontal component is zero and a ratio with zero in the denominator is mathematically impossible. A line with a very large slope (for example, 1,000,000) is almost vertical.

Planning You may want to discuss the Summary and have students reflect on the concept of slope. Students may work on problems **20** and **21** individually. These problems may also be used as informal assessments. After students finish Section C, you may assign appropriate activities from the Try This! section, located on pages 45–49 of the *Graphing Equations* Student Book, for homework.

Comments about the Problems

20–21. Informal Assessment These problems assess students' ability to understand the meaning of slope in different contexts and to understand the graph of a line in the coordinate plane.

20. A line is determined by two points. There is only one line that can pass through both of two given points.

SECTION D. AN EQUATION OF A LINE

Work Students Do

Students use the direction of a line (described with a number pair) to explore how a line is drawn. They explain why lines on computer screens are sometimes smooth and sometimes jagged. Then students are introduced to the equation of a line, with a starting point and a slope. Students interpret the meanings of numbers in equations, and draw the lines described by equations. They describe the steepness of a line by measuring the angle the line makes with the x-axis. Students see that the tangent of that angle is the same as the slope of the line.

Goals

Students will:

- describe and graph directions using angles;*
- find and use equations of the form $y = i + sx$ using the slope and y-intercept;
- graph equations of the form $y = i + sx$;
- understand the meaning of slope in different contexts;*
- understand the graph of a line in the coordinate plane;
- model a problem situation and translate it to a graph or an equation.*

   * These goals are assessed in other sections of the unit.

Pacing

- approximately three 45-minute class sessions

Vocabulary

- equation of a line
- intercept
- tangent

About the Mathematics

One way to write the equation of a line is $y = i + sx$, where the variable i is the y-intercept and the variable s is the slope of the line. (Traditionally, the equation is written in the form $y = mx + b$, where the variable m is the slope and the variable b is the y-intercept.) The variable i, or y-intercept, is the place where the line crosses the y-axis. Algebraically, the y-value of the equation equals i when the x-value is 0. The variable s is the slope of the line, and tells how steep the line is.

The tangent of the angle that a line makes with the positive (or right) side of the x-axis is equal to the slope because the tangent of an angle is defined as the vertical distance divided by the horizontal distance. Students were introduced to this concept in the grade 7/8 unit *Looking at an Angle*.

Students develop many skills in this section. They find the equation of a line from the graph of a line, graph a line given its equation, create an equation from a situation, and use angles to find slopes.

Materials

- graphing calculators, with tangent function keys, pages 57, 61, 63, 65, and 69 of the Teacher Guide (one per student or per class)

- overhead projector, pages 57 and 63 of the Teacher Guide, optional (one per class)

- graph paper, pages 67 and 69 of the Teacher Guide (one sheet per student)

- protractors or compass cards, pages 67 and 69 of the Teacher Guide (one per student)

- rulers, page 69 of the Teacher Guide (one per student)

Planning Instruction

You may want to introduce this section by demonstrating how to use a graphing calculator to draw lines. Graph a line and have students examine exactly how a line is formed by the graphing calculator. Rather than drawing a straight line, the graphing calculator actually turns on a series of pixels that lie along a straight line. It is easy to see the jagged edges of the line. You might have students consider whether there is a relationship between the slope of a graphed line and the way the pixels are presented on the screen.

Students may work on problems 1 and 2 as a whole class. They may do problems 3–6 in small groups. The remaining problems may be done individually.

Problems 9c, 16, 17a, and 18–23 are optional. Problems 9c, 16, and 17a require graphing calculators. If you do not have graphing calculators, you may omit these problems or have students draw these graphs on graph paper. Problems 18–23 refer to work students did in the grade 7/8 unit *Looking at an Angle*. If time is a concern or if students have not worked on *Looking at an Angle,* you may omit these problems.

Homework

Problems 11 and 12 (page 62 of the Teacher Guide), 13 and 14 (page 64 of the Teacher Guide), and 24 and 25 (page 70 of the Teacher Guide) may be assigned as homework. The Extension activities (pages 61 and 65 of the Teacher Guide) and the Bringing Math Home activity (page 59 of the Teacher Guide) may also be assigned as homework. After students finish Section D, you may assign appropriate activities from the Try This! section located on pages 45–49 of the *Graphing Equations* Student Book. The Try This! activities reinforce the key mathematical concepts introduced in this section.

Planning Assessment

- Problems 8, 13, 14, and 24 can be used to informally assess students' ability to find and use equations of the form $y = i + sx$ using the slope and y-intercept.

- Problem 25 can be used to informally assess students' ability to find and use equations of the form $y = i + sx$ using the slope and y-intercept, graph equations of the form $y = i + sx$, and their ability to understand the graph of a line in the coordinate plane.

D. AN EQUATION OF A LINE

Stepping on a Line

If you look closely at a line on a computer screen, you can see that the screen is made up of pixels, or dots.

1. Explain why sometimes a line on a computer screen is smooth and sometimes it is jagged.

2. Below is a computer-drawn line in the direction [+1, +2] from *B*. Explain how you can tell that the direction of the line is [+1, +2].

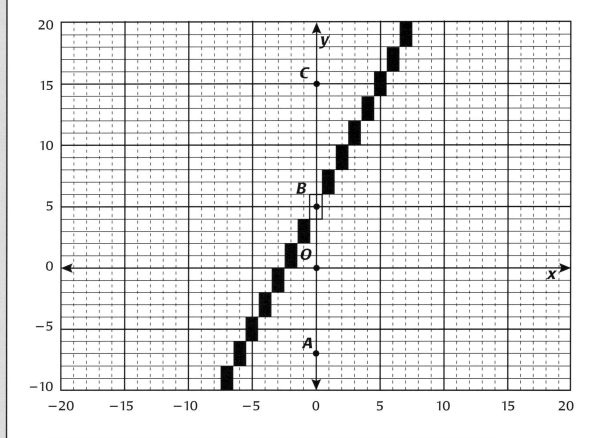

You can think of moving along the line one step at a time. Each step is a move of +1 unit horizontally and + 2 units vertically.

(0, 5)
+1 ⇓ ⇓+2
(1, 7)
+1 ⇓ ⇓+2
(2, 9) etc.

3. a. The description on the right shows two steps. Where are you after 10 steps?

b. Where are you after 25 steps? After 1,000 steps?

1. Explanations will vary. Sample explanations:

Pixels are different sizes, depending on the resolution of the computer monitor.

2. Answers will vary. Sample responses:

The middle of each box shifts one to the right and up two.

The boxes on the screen have the dimensions that are one unit by two units.

3. a. You are at (10, 25) after 10 steps

   b. You are at (25, 55) after 25 steps, and (1,000, 2,005) after 1,000 steps.

Materials graphing calculator (or computer graphing software), optional (one per class); overhead projector, optional (one per class)

Overview Students investigate how a computer draws straight lines, and how a straight line can be drawn by taking the same steps each time.

About the Mathematics A straight line is actually a collection of an infinite number of points. Theoretically, the points themselves have no dimensions, and the line has no thickness. In practice, however, a line does have a thickness and a point does have dimensions. When a computer (or graphing calculator) draws a line, it plots a large number of points (called pixels) that form a line. Whether the points can be identified or not, depends on the resolution of the screen.

Planning Students may work on problems **1** and **2** as a whole class. They may do problem **3** in small groups.

Comments about the Problems

1. Students should think about this question carefully, but they are not expected to come up with accurate answers.

2. You may wish to draw the line shown on page 23 of the Student Book with an overhead graphing calculator or computer graphing software so that students can see the line as it is created with pixels. The equation of the line shown on page 23 of the Student Book is $y = 5 + 2x$. As students work on this section, you may want to use the TABLE feature on the calculator to replicate the tables in the Teacher Guide and verify the answers.

3. b. Students might complete the sequence 5, 7, 9, 11, . . . 25. This will be more difficult for 1,000 steps. Students will have to think of a formula or pattern. One possible pattern is as follows: Since you add two vertically for each step, after 1,000 steps you have $2 \times 1,000 = 2,000$. Then you have to add the five you started with to arrive at a total of 2,005.

The description on the right shows steps in the opposite direction.

$$(0, 5)$$
−1 ⇓ ⇓ −2
$$(-1, 3)$$
−1 ⇓ ⇓ −2
$$(-2, 1)$$ etc.

4. a. Where are you after 10 steps?

b. After 100 steps?

A computer can quickly calculate and draw all the points in problems **3** and **4.** The graph on the right is still not a smooth line. The pixels are still too large.

5. What can you do to make the graph look more like a smooth line?

6. Suppose the computer takes horizontal steps of +0.1 and −0.1 when drawing the points in problems **3** and **4.**

a. What are the corresponding vertical distances for each step?

b. If you start at (0, 5), where are you after 8 steps with +0.1 as the horizontal distance?

c. If you start at (0, 5), Where are you after 3 steps using −0.1 as the horizontal distance?

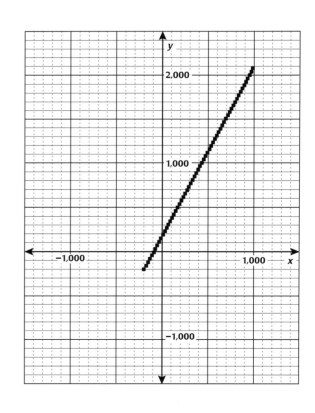

4. a. (−10, −15)

   b. (−100, −195)

5. take smaller steps

6. a. +0.2 and −0.2

   b. (0.8, 6.6). Strategies will vary. Sample strategy: Complete eight steps of +0.1 and +0.2.

   c. (−0.3, 4.4)

Overview Students calculate points that are on a line.

Planning Students may work on problems **4–6** in small groups.

Comments about the Problems

   5. Students should be able to do these problems without a graphing calculator.

   6. After students finish problem **6,** you may want to discuss their answers and ask students what rule they can formulate based on their calculations.

Bringing Math Home You may want to ask students who have a computer at home to draw a line, describe what it looks like on the screen, print it, and bring the description and the printout to class. Then, you can discuss the descriptions and printouts as a class.

7. Here is a rule you may have discovered:

Starting point: (0, 5).
After 100 horizontal steps of +1:

$$x = 100$$
$$y = 5 + 100 \times 2 = 205$$

a. Write a similar rule for 75 horizontal steps of +1.

b. Write a rule for 175 horizontal steps of +1.

c. Do the same for $3\frac{1}{2}$ horizontal steps of +1.

From the rules you wrote in problem **7,** you can find a formula relating the *x*-coordinates and the *y*-coordinates:

$$y = 5 + x \cdot 2 \quad \text{or} \quad y = 5 + 2x$$

8. a. Explain the formula.

   b. Does the formula work for negative values of *x*?

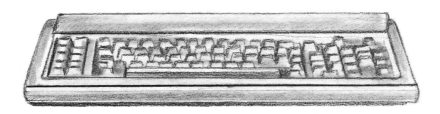

7. **a.** After 75 horizontal steps of $+1$,

$x = 75$
$y = 5 + 75 \times 2 = 155$

b. $x = 175$
$y = 5 + 175 \times 2 = 355$

c. $x = 3.5$
$y = 5 + 3.5 \times 2 = 12$

8. **a.** Explanations will vary. Sample explanation:

The y-coordinate is equal to two times the x-coordinate plus five.

b. yes

Materials graphing calculators, optional (one per student)

Overview Students write rules to describe how particular straight lines are drawn.

About the Mathematics The rule for a straight line that is introduced on page 25 of the Student Book is the equation of a line. However, on this page, the rule is used only as a generalized calculation rule, as students used formulas in the grade 6/7 unit *Expressions and Formulas*.

Planning Students may work on problems **7** and **8** individually. Problem **8** can also be used as an informal assessment.

Comments about the Problems

8. **Informal Assessment** This problem assesses students' ability to find and use equations of the form $y = i + sx$ using the slope and y-intercept.

Problem **8** is critical because students are asked to make a connection between an algebraic rule and the graph of a line.

Extension Using the graphing calculator, have students use the TRACE feature to investigate the actual pixels used to create a line. You might also have them use the TABLE feature along with TBLSET to generate a table of values that match the TRACE step.

The formula $y = 5 + 2x$ is called an *equation of a line.* If you enter an equation of a line into a graphing calculator (or other graphing software), the display shows a line.

Instruction: Y = 5 + 2X
Result:

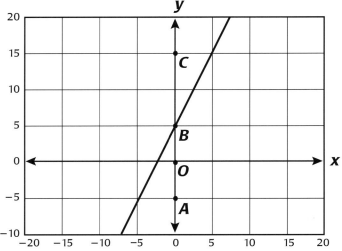

9. In the instruction Y = 5 + 2X, two numbers play special roles.

    a. What is the importance of the "5" for the graph?

    b. What is the importance of the "2" for the graph?

    c. Use a graphing calculator to show $y = 5 + 2x$. Explain how to change the window of your calculator to display the same range of *x*-values and *y*-values as shown above.

There are special names for the "5" and the "2" in the equation $y = 5 + 2x$.
The "5" is called the *y-intercept.*

10. Why do you think it is called the *y*-intercept?

11. Write the instruction for a line that goes through point *C* and has a slope 2.

12. Make a copy of the graph shown above on a piece of graph paper.

    a. Show the line through *B* with slope $\frac{1}{2}$. Then label the line with its equation.

    b. Show the line through *C* with slope $\frac{1}{2}$ and label the line with its equation.

    c. What do you notice about the two lines? Justify your answer.

9. a. The "5" is where the line crosses the y-axis.

b. The "2" is the slope. You move two units vertically for every one unit horizontally.

c. $y_1 = 5 + 2x$

x max $= 20$

x min $= -20$

x scl $= 5$

y max $= 20$

y min $= -20$

y scl $= 5$

10. The y-intercept is the value of y where the line crosses, or intercepts, the y-axis.

11. $y = 15 + 2x$

12.

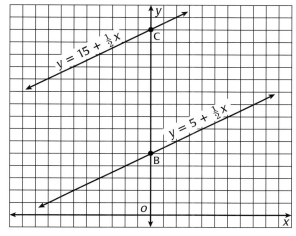

a. $y = 5 + \frac{1}{2}x$

b. $y = 15 + \frac{1}{2}x$

c. They are parallel. They have the same slope and different y-intercepts, so they will never meet.

Materials graphing calculators (one per student); overhead projector, optional (one per class)

Overview Students are introduced to the equation of a line (using slope and y-intercept).

About the Mathematics The equation of a straight line is often given as $y = mx + b$. *Mathematics in Context* units use the notation $y = i + sx$, or $y = sx + i$, where i stands for the y-intercept, and s for the slope. The y-intercept is the value of y where the line crosses the y-axis. This value is also called the *starting point*.

Planning Students may work on problems **9–12** individually. You may want to introduce this page with a demonstration on the overhead, using a graphing calculator if you have one. Problem **9c** is optional. If you do not have graphing calculators available, you may omit this problem. Problems **11** and **12** may be assigned as homework.

Comments about the Problems

9–10. These problems are critical because students are asked to make a connection between an algebraic rule and the graph of a line. If students have difficulty using the viewing windows on their graphing calculators, you might suggest that they refer to the graph on page 26 of the Student Book. Encourage students to describe the meanings of "5" and "2" in their own words. Discuss which descriptions make sense and why.

10. If students have difficulty, you might remind them of the use of the term *interception* in football.

11–12. Homework These problems may be assigned as homework.

13. These two equations represent the same line:

$$y = 5 + (-2) \cdot x \qquad \text{or} \qquad y = 5 - 2x$$

Explain why the equations represent the line through *B* with slope −2.

14. **a.** Write an equation for the line through *C* with slope $-\frac{1}{4}$.

b. Write an equation for the line through *A* with slope −1.

15. **a.** Write an equation for the line that contains *B* and forms a 45° angle with the direction east.

b. What is the equation if the line contains *O* instead of *B?*

16. Make three lines on a graphing calculator. Show them to a partner. Have the partner write an equation for each line.

17. **a.** Use your graphing calculator to display the six lines shown on the left. In your notebook, write the equation for each of the six lines.

b. Which lines are parallel? Explain your answers.

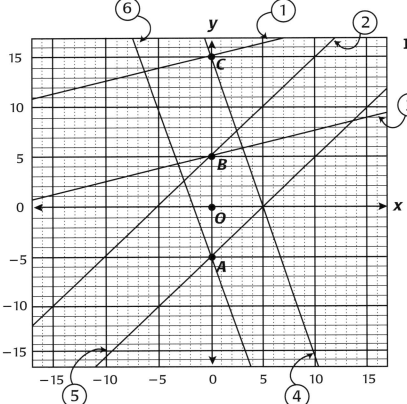

13. The line passes through point B (0, 5). The slope of -2 means that the vertical component is -2 when the horizontal component is $+1$, so the equation of the line is $y = 5 + -2x$.

14. a. $y = 15 - \frac{1}{4}x$ or $y = 15 + (\frac{1}{4})x$

   b. $y = -5 - 1x$ or $y = -5 - x$

15. a. $y = 5 + 1x$, or $y = 5 + x$

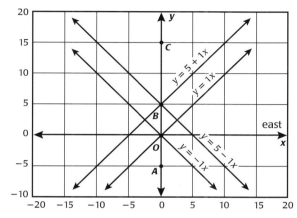

   b. $y = 0 + 1x \ (y = x)$

   See graph above.

16. Answers will vary, depending on students' lines.

17. a. equation 1: $y = 15 + \frac{1}{4}x$

   equation 2: $y = 5 + x$

   equation 3: $y = 5 + \frac{1}{4}x$

   equation 4: $y = 15 - 3x$

   equation 5: $y = -5 + x$

   equation 6: $y = -5 - 3x$

   b. The following lines are parallel: 1 and 3; 2 and 5; 4 and 6. Each pair of lines has the same slope.

Materials graphing calculators (one per student)

Overview Students write equations for lines and display lines using graphing calculators.

About the Mathematics There are several ways to find the equation of a line. At this point, it is sufficient for students to use the strategy of finding the y-intercept (from the graph), finding the slope, and writing the equation of the line. Lines are parallel if their slopes are the same.

Planning Students may work on problems **13–17** individually. Problems **16** and **17a** are optional. If you do not have graphing calculators, you may omit these problems. Problems **13** and **14** may be assigned as homework or used as informal assessments.

Comments about the Problems

13–14. Informal Assessment These problems assess students' ability to find and use equations of the form $y = i + sx$ using the slope and y-intercept. These problems may also be assigned as homework.

17. b. Students may have difficulty finding the slope of each of these lines because they need to find points with easy-to-read coordinates. The right ends of lines 1, 2, 3, and 5 each leave the grid at an easy-to-read point. You may want to suggest that students use the coordinates of these points to find the slopes.

Extension You may want to have students write the equations for the lines in some of the graphs from previous sections of this unit.

What's the Angle?

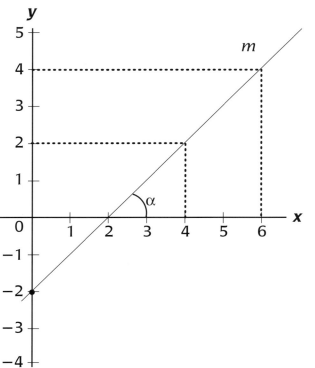

In the unit *Looking At An Angle,* you used the measure of an angle to describe the slope of a line.

18. a. What is the slope of line *m*? What is its *y*-intercept?

b. Write an equation for line *m*.

c. Using graph paper, draw line *m*. Then draw another line through (2, 0) whose slope is twice that of line *m*.

19. a. Measure angle α (the Greek letter "alpha") in the graph above. Then measure the same angle in your graph to be sure the angles are the same size.

b. What is the measure of the angle formed by your new line?

c. Is there a relationship between the two angles? If so, explain that relationship.

18. a. The slope is 1, and the *y*-intercept is −2.

   b. $y = -2 + x$

   c.

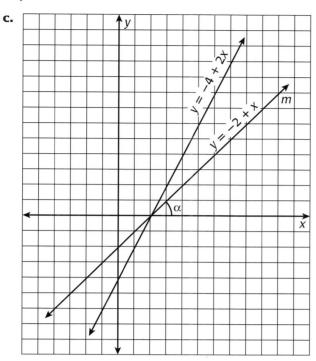

19. a. 45°

   b. about 63°

   c. Explanations will vary. Sample explanation:

   The second angle is larger, but not twice as large.

Materials graph paper (one sheet per student); protractors or compass cards (one per student)

Overview Students relate the slope of a line to the angle the line makes with the *x*-axis.

About the Mathematics The tangent of the angle a line makes with the positive *x*-axis is the same as the slope of the line. The slope is not proportional to the angle; an angle that is twice as large does not correspond to a slope that is twice as large.

Planning Students may work on problems **18** and **19** individually. These problems are optional. They refer to material students learned in the grade 7/8 unit *Looking at an Angle*. If time is a concern, or students have not worked on *Looking at an Angle*, you may omit these problems.

Comments about the Problems

19. Students should use a protractor or compass card to measure and draw the angles. They should only measure the size of the angle formed with the right side of the *x*-axis.

You probably noticed in problem **19** that the size of the angle did not double when the slope of the line doubled.

20. a. Draw two lines on graph paper, one that forms a 30° angle with the *x*-axis and one that forms a 60° angle with the *x*-axis.

   b. Estimate the slope of each line.

There is an angle that corresponds to every slope. The slope is equal to the *tangent ratio* for that angle, abbreviated *tan*.

$$\textbf{slope} = \textbf{tan}\,\alpha = \frac{\textbf{vertical component}}{\textbf{horizontal component}}$$

21. Find the slope and tangent ratio for each of the lines shown at the right.

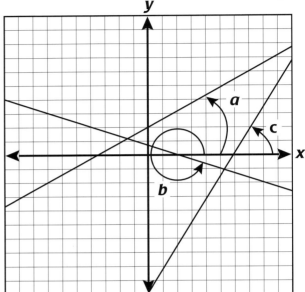

Most scientific calculators have a tangent key (TAN). Given either the slope of the line or the angle formed by the line and the *x*-axis, the tangent key enables you to find the other value.

22. Measure the three angles above. Using the tangent key on a scientific calculator, check your answers to problem **21.**

23. The line shown on the left forms two angles. The line has a slope of −1 so tan α = −1. Use the tangent key on a scientific calculator to decide which angle represents angle α.

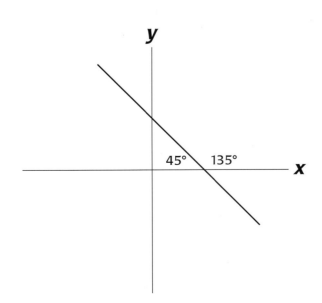

20. a. Lines may vary, depending on their *y*-intercepts. Sample graph:

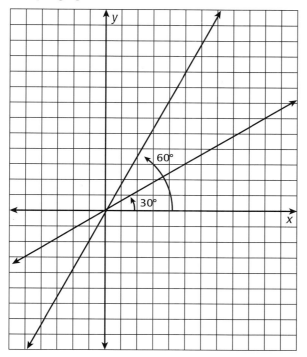

b. Estimates will vary. Sample estimates:

Slope of the 30° line: $\frac{6}{10}$

Slope of 60° line: $\frac{9}{5}$

21. $\tan a = \text{slope} = \frac{4}{7}$
$\tan b = \text{slope} = -\frac{1}{3}$
$\tan c = \text{slope} = \frac{5}{3}$

22. $\tan a = \frac{4}{7}$, $a = 29.7°$
$\tan b = -\frac{1}{3}$, $b = 161.5°$
$\tan c = \frac{5}{3}$, $c = 59°$

Note: On the graph on Teacher Guide page 68, the arc drawn for the angle between line *b* and the horizontal axis should stop at line *b*.

23. $\alpha = -45°$ or $135°$

Materials graphing calculators (one per student); graph paper (one sheet per student); protractors or compass cards (one per student); rulers (one per student)

Overview Students continue to investigate the relationship between slope and tangent.

About the Mathematics The mathematics on this page is related to the work students did in the grade 7/8 unit *Looking at an Angle.* The convention in mathematics is always to measure the angle with the positive (or right) part of the *x*-axis, to avoid confusion about what angle to deal with.

Planning Students may work on problems **20–23** individually. These problems are optional. They refer to material students learned in the grade 7/8 unit *Looking at an Angle.* If time is a concern, or students have not worked on *Looking at an Angle,* you may omit these problems.

Comments about the Problems

20. b. Students estimate the slope of each line rather than find the exact slopes. One strategy is to compare the lines to lines with a slope the students know. A sophisticated strategy is to find a point where the lines cross the grid and use it to estimate the slope. For example, the line at a 60° angle crosses the grid at about (4, 9). This gives a vertical component (measured from 0) of 7, and a horizontal component of 4. The estimate for the slope would therefore be $\frac{7}{4} = 1.75$

Summary

Equation of a line

An equation for the line that contains the point (0, 5) and has slope 3 is

$$y = 5 + 3x$$

The number 5 indicates the intercept on the y-axis.

The number 3 is the value of the slope.

The equation of a line that is not vertical has this form:

$y = \text{intercept} + \text{slope} \cdot x$
$y = i + sx$ where
$i = y\text{-intercept}$ and $s = \text{slope}$.

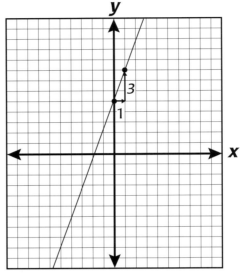

Another way to describe the slope is using a tangent ratio:

$$\text{slope} = \tan \alpha = \frac{\textbf{vertical component}}{\textbf{horizontal component}}$$

Summary Questions

The y-intercept of a line may be positive, zero, or negative. Also, the slope of a line may be positive, zero, or negative.

24. Explain why there are nine combinations for the values of the y-intercept and the slope of a line.

25. Write an example for each combination in problem **24** and show a graph of each example.

Solutions and Samples
of student work

24. Each of the three values of *i* can be combined with three possibilities for *s* (3 × 3 = 9).

25. Answers will vary. Sample lines and graphs:

$y = 5 + 2x$
$y = 5 + 0x = 5$
$y = 5 - 2x$

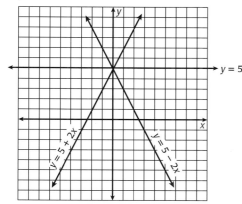

$y = -5 + 2x$
$y = -5 + 0x = -5$
$y = -5 - 2x$

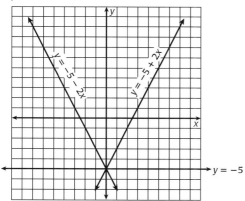

$y = 0 + 2x = 2x$
$y = 0 + 0x = 0$ (the *x*-axis)
$y = 0 - 2x = -2x$

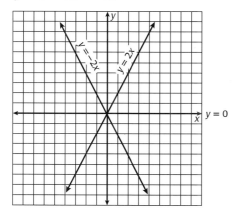

Hints and Comments

Overview Students read the Summary, which reviews the main concepts covered in this section. They reflect on the equation of a line, the meaning of the *y*-intercept, and the slope.

About the Mathematics The notation used in the Summary for the equation of a line is referred to as the slope intercept form. In mathematics, the general equation of a line is often written as $y = mx + b$. This is, of course, the same as $y = i + sx$. Vertical lines have no slope and their equations are of the form $x = a$, where *a* is some constant.

Planning Students may work on problems **24** and **25** individually. These problems can also be assigned as homework or used as informal assessments. After students finish Section D, you may assign appropriate activities from the Try This! section, located on pages 45–49 of the *Graphing Equations* Student Book, for homework.

Comments about the Problems

24–25. Homework These problems may be assigned as homework. Before students complete these problems, you may want to discuss the Summary and to mention that there are several ways to write the equation of a line.

24. Informal Assessment This problem assesses students' ability to find and use equations of the form $y = i + sx$ using the slope and *y*-intercept.

25. Informal Assessment This problem assesses students' ability to find and use equations of the form $y = i + sx$ using the slope and *y*-intercept, graph equations of the form $y = i + sx$, and understand the graph of a line in the coordinate plane.

SECTION E. SOLVING EQUATIONS

Work Students Do

Students meet Alice and Fred, two frogs who are jumping away from a path. Students consider what information they would need to determine Alice and Fred's new distances from the path. Students use diagrams to help them solve problems about the lengths of the frogs' jumps and the distances the frogs travel. Then students move from diagrams to number lines. In this context, students learn to solve equations of the form $a + bx = c + dx$. In these problems, the unknown x is the length of each frog's jump. Students also write and solve frog problems of their own.

Goals

Students will:

- solve equations of the form $a + bx = c + dx$;

- understand how to find the intersection point of two lines, algebraically;*

- model a problem situation and translate it to a graph or an equation;

- choose an appropriate way to solve equations;

- understand the similarities between graphic and algebraic strategies.*

  * These goals are assessed in other sections of the unit.

Pacing

- approximately three to four 45-minute class sessions

Vocabulary

- unknown

About the Mathematics

In an equation, the same number can be added or subtracted from both sides without changing the answer (the x-value). Also, the same number can be multiplied or divided from both sides without changing the answer.

Box diagrams can be used to visualize equations. Below is a diagram for the equation $14 + 2x = 6 + 5x$.

Materials

- blank transparency, page 75 of the Teacher Guide, optional (one per class)
- overhead projector, page 75 of the Teacher Guide, optional (one per class)
- centimeter rulers, page 77 of the Teacher Guide (one per student)

Planning Instruction

You may want to introduce this section with a discussion of frogs. Most frogs have strong back legs that they use for swimming and jumping. Ask students, *How far do you think a frog can jump compared to its body length?* [On a level surface, the average frog can jump a length that is about 20 times the length of its body.]

Students may work on problem 1 as a class. They may work on problems 2–3 and 14–15 in small groups. The remaining problems may be done individually.

There are no optional problems in this section.

Homework

Problems 11 and 12 (page 80 of the Teacher Guide), and problems 19, 20, and 21 (page 88 of the Teacher Guide) may be assigned as homework. The Extension (page 89 of the Teacher Guide) and the Writing Opportunity (page 89 of the Teacher Guide) may also be assigned as homework. After students finish Section E, you may assign appropriate activities from the Try This! section, located on pages 45–49 of the *Graphing Equations* Student Book. The Try This! activities reinforce the key mathematical concepts introduced in this section.

Planning Assessment

- Problem 13 can be used to informally assess students' ability to solve equations of the form $a + bx = c + dx$.
- Problem 19 can be used to informally assess students' ability to solve equations of the form $a + bx = c + dx$, and to model a problem situation and translate it to a graph or an equation.
- Problems 20 and 21 can be used to informally assess students' ability to solve equations of the form $a + bx = c + dx$.
- Problem 24 can be used to informally assess students' ability to solve equations of the form $a + bx = c + dx$, and choose an appropriate way to solve equations.
- Problem 25 can be used to informally assess students' ability to solve equations of the form $a + bx = c + dx$, and to model a problem situation and translate it to a graph or an equation. It also assesses their ability to choose an appropriate way to solve equations.

E. SOLVING EQUATIONS

JUMPING TO CONCLUSIONS

The activities in the previous sections involved coordinates and directions. The activities led to investigating the slope and equation of a line. This section takes a look at writing and solving equations.

Two frogs, Alice and Fred, are near a path in a forest. Suddenly they hear footsteps on the path. To avoid possible danger, they jump away from the path.

Alice begins 8 decimeters (dm) from the path, and Fred begins 18 decimeters from the path (10 decimeters = 1 meter). Each takes several jumps, then stops.

1. What information would you need to find their new distances from the path?

1. You need to know how long a jump is, how many jumps each frog makes, and the directions of the jumps.

Materials blank transparency, optional (one per class); overhead projector, optional (one per class)

Overview Students meet Alice and Fred, two frogs who are jumping away from a path. Students consider what information they would need to find the frogs' new distances from the path.

About the Mathematics In the previous sections, students found the point of intersection of two lines graphically, reading the coordinates on the coordinate grid system. In this section, a formal method for finding the point of intersection by solving equations will be developed. This process of solving equations is useful in many other algebraic problems as well.

Planning Students may work on problem **1** as a class.

Comments about the Problems

1. You may want to introduce this section by telling the story about the jumping frogs and drawing the situation on an overhead projector or a blackboard. Draw a path as the starting point, and indicate the position where each frog starts jumping. Make clear that the frogs jump perpendicular to the path. You can use strips of equal length to indicate the jumps.

Suppose that Alice and Fred travel the same distance with each jump, but Alice takes 5 jumps and Fred takes 3 jumps. The diagram below illustrates their new positions.

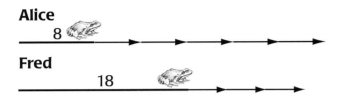

Alice

    8

Fred

        18

2. a. Suppose Alice and Fred travel 4 decimeters with each jump. Find the distance from the path to each frog's new position. Draw a diagram showing this situation.

   b. Suppose you know that each jump is between 2 decimeters and 6 decimeters. What can you conclude about where each frog finishes?

Suppose the frogs finish their jumps at exactly the same distance from the path, and you want to know the distance of each jump and each frog's final distance from the path. In groups, discuss strategies for solving this problem.

3. Share your group's method with the other members of your class.

2. a. Alice will be 28 dm from the path and Fred will be 30 dm from the path.

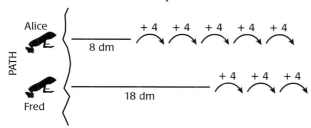

b. The following is a jump-by-jump summary of different possible jump lengths:

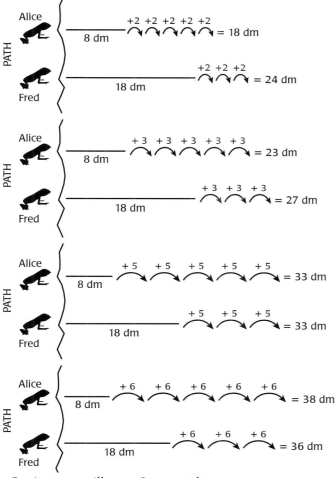

3. Answers will vary. Some students may say that 8 decimeters + n jumps should equal 18 decimeters + m jumps, where n is the number of jumps for Alice, and m is the number of jumps for Fred. The jumps should all be the same length. The following are two possible ways to solve this problem:

• Choose a value for the length of a jump and then find m and n.

• Choose values for m and n and then find the length of a jump.

Materials centimeter rulers (one per student)

Overview Students consider the effects of different jump lengths on the total distance each frog jumps.

About the Mathematics The distance each frog jumps from the path depends on the starting position, the length of a jump, and the number of jumps. The distance jumped is called the dependent variable, because it depends on other variables. When the starting distance and the number of jumps are fixed, the only variable left is the length of a jump. It is common in mathematics to use a letter to represent a variable. Any letter can be used, but often the letter x is chosen. In the frog problems, the relationship between the dependent variable and the other variables can be written as follows: total distance = starting distance + number of jumps × length. This is a linear relationship.

Planning Students may work on problems **2** and **3** in small groups.

Comments about the Problems

2. The starting distances are the same in both situations. You may want to remind students to draw the diagrams to scale. For example, one centimeter could equal one decimeter. If so, the starting distance for Alice would be 4 centimeters, and for Fred, 9 centimeters. The jumps should also be drawn to scale, so students can measure their drawings to find the distance of each new position.

3. At this point, students may start to use shortcuts to describe situations. They may use letters to indicate the number of jumps and the length of jumps.

One way to answer problem **3** is to label the *unknown.* In this problem, the unknown is the length of each jump. You can use the symbol *x* for the length of a jump. The box below gives a diagram and an equation for answering problem **3**.

Box A

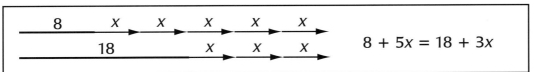

$$8 + 5x = 18 + 3x$$

4. Explain how the equation $8 + 5x = 18 + 3x$ describes the diagram in Box A.

As steps in finding the length of a jump, look at the following diagrams and equations.

5. Explain the equation in Box B and describe how the diagram was changed from Box A to Box B.

Box B

$$8 + 2x = 18$$

6. Explain the equation in Box C and describe how the diagram was changed from Box B to Box C.

Box C

$$2x = 10$$

7. Explain the equation in Box D and describe how the diagram was changed from Box C to Box D.

Box D

$$x = \tfrac{10}{2} = 5$$

4. Explanations will vary. Some students may explain that the expression $8 + 5x$ represents the total distance Alice jumped. She started at 8 decimeters and took five jumps of length x. The expression $18 + 3x$ represents the total distance Fred jumped. He started at 18 decimeters and took three jumps of length x. If both Alice and Fred end up at the same distance from the path, the two expressions must be equal.

5. Three jumps have been taken away from each frog.

6. Eight decimeters have been taken away from each frog's starting distance.

7. If two jumps equal 10 decimeters, then each jump equals $10 \div 2 = 5$ decimeters.

Overview Students explore diagrams and equations that describe the frog jumps, and analyze one strategy for solving an equation.

About the Mathematics On the previous pages, the length of the jumps and the number of jumps were variable. From here on, the length of the jump remains fixed for each situation, but continues to be an unknown length. In the rest of this section, the number of jumps and the starting distance will be given. Because it is also given that the two frogs end at the same distance from the path, the situation is now completely fixed. The students' task is to find the value of the unknown length of a jump.

The total length is not variable, since there is only one value for which the equation is true. This unknown value (the length of the jump) can be represented with the letter x. Later in this unit, students will relate the equations representing frog jumps to the equations of a line.

Planning Students may work on problems **4–7** individually. You may want to discuss their answers.

Comments about the Problems

4. The left side of the equation represents the total distance traveled by one frog, and the right side of the equation, the total distance traveled by the second frog. Students may want to label each side of the equation with the name of the corresponding frog.

This problem is critical because it is the first time that the representation of equations with arrows is introduced. It is important that students understand this notation so that they can fall back on it whenever they are solving equations.

5–7. Encourage students to describe the steps taken from box to box in their own words.

Write a "frog problem" and an expression to represent each diagram in problems **8** and **9**.

8.

$$\underline{\qquad 10 \qquad} \; x \;, \; x \;, \; x \;, \; x \;,$$

9.

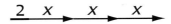

$$\underline{2} \; x \;, \; x \;, \; x \;,$$

10. a. Write a "frog problem" and an equation to represent the diagram in Box A below.

Box A

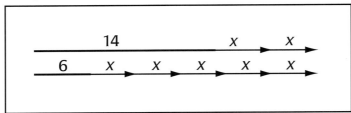

b. Draw the diagram for the next step in finding the value of x and write the equation for your diagram.

c. Complete the sequence of diagrams and equations.

11. Here is an equation: $12 + 2x = 6 + 4x$.

a. Use a sequence of boxes to solve the equation. Start by drawing a diagram to represent each side of the equation.

b. Draw the rest of the boxes and diagrams to solve the equation.

12. a. Describe the equation $11 + 9x = 26 + 4x$ as a "frog problem."

b. Find the value of x in the equation and explain the steps of your solution. You may want to use a series of boxes, diagrams, and equations as part of your explanation.

13. Solve each equation for its unknown value and explain your method. How can you be sure that your answers are correct?

a. $100 + w + w = 75 + w + w + w + w$

b. $y + 42 + y = 12 + 3y + 2y$

c. $144 + z = 120 + 9z$

8. Problems will vary. Sample problem:

A frog starts 10 decimeters from the path and takes four jumps of the same length. The diagram can be represented by the following expression: $10 + 4x$.

9. Problems will vary. Sample problem:

A frog starts 2 decimeters from the path and takes three jumps of the same length. The diagram can be represented by the following expression: $2 + 3x$.

10. a. Problems will vary. Sample problem:

Alice starts 14 decimeters from the path and takes two jumps. Fred starts 6 decimeters from the path and takes five jumps. They end up at the same distance from the path.

$$6 + 5x = 14 + 2x$$

b.

$$14 = 6 + 3x$$

c.

$$8 = 3x; \ x = 8 \div 3 = 2\tfrac{2}{3} \text{ decimeters}$$

11. a–b.

$$12 = 6 + 2x$$
$$6 = 2x$$
$$x = 6 \div 2 = 3$$

12. a. Descriptions will vary. Sample description:

One frog starts 11 decimeters from the path and takes nine equal jumps. Another frog starts 26 decimeters from the path and takes four equal jumps. They both end up an equal distance from the path.

b. The value of x is 3 decimeters. Strategies will vary. Sample strategy:

Solving for x:
$$11 + 9x = 26 + 4x$$
$$11 + 5x = 26$$
$$5x = 15$$
$$x = \tfrac{15}{5} = 3$$

Note: See the solution column on Teacher Guide page 83 for the solution to problem **13.**

Overview Students write some frog problems. They also draw diagrams and write equations.

About the Mathematics Students may use the box diagram to visualize the equation. The diagrams are drawn to scale, allowing for another solution strategy—measuring the length of x and multiplying it by the scale factor. It may be helpful for students to use this measuring strategy once, so they will recognize the meaning of the visual model.

Planning Students may work on problems **8–13** individually. Problems **11** and **12** may be assigned as homework, and problem **13** can be used as an informal assessment.

Comments about the Problems

10. Problem **10** combines two equations and is similar to problems **4–7,** on page 33 of the Student Book. Although the lengths 6, 14, and x are drawn to scale on page 34 of the Student Book, students do not necessarily need to make their drawings to scale as well. When students understand that the boxes and diagrams are sketches to help them visualize the equation, they should realize that the scale is not important.

After students complete these problems, they should start to understand how to solve an equation using a box and an equation to describe each step of the process.

11–12. Homework These problems may be assigned as homework. When students feel comfortable solving the problems without drawing the boxes, let them do so, but make sure they can explain each step of their solutions.

13. Informal Assessment This problem assesses students' ability to solve equations of the form $a + bx = c + dx$. Students should recognize that these problems are formulated in a slightly different way from the previous problems.

a. Students should recognize that $w + w = 2w$.

b. Students should recognize that $y + 42 + y = 42 + 2y$ and that $3y + 2y = 5y$.

One day, while exploring their territory, Alice is 14 decimeters from the pond and Fred is 50 decimeters from the pond. They start jumping toward each other. As shown below, they met after Fred took four jumps toward Alice and Alice took six jumps toward Fred.

Opposites *Attract*

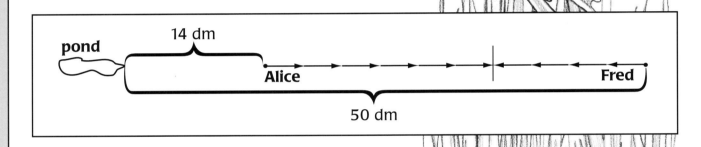

Box A

$$14 + 6x = 50 - 4x$$

Box B

$$14 + 10x = 50$$

14. Suppose both frogs travel the same distance *x* with each jump.

    a. Explain how the diagram and equation in Box A represent the frogs' positions.

    b. Explain the equation in Box B, and describe how the diagram was changed from Box A to Box B.

Solutions and Samples
of student work

13. a.

100
w w
75
w w w w
100
75
w w
25
w w

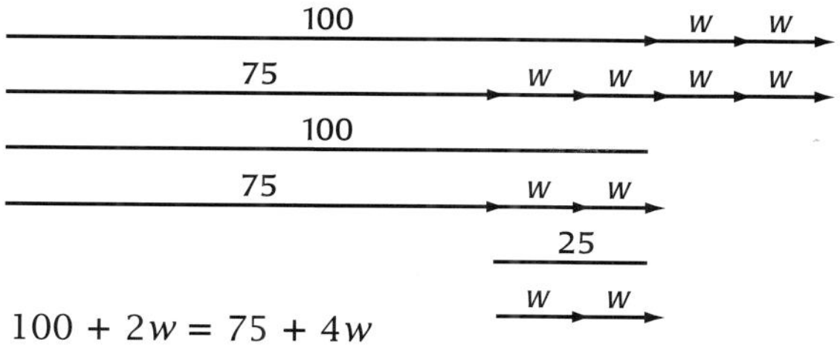

$100 + 2w = 75 + 4w$
$100 = 75 + 2w$
$25 = 2w$
$w = 12.5$

b. $42 + 2y = 12 + 5y$
$42 = 12 + 3y$
$30 = 3y$
$y = 30 \div 3 = 10$

c. $144 + z = 120 + 9z$
$144 = 120 + 8z$
$24 = 8z$
$24 \div 8 = z$
$z = 3$

14. a. Explanations will vary. Sample explanation:

The first diagram shows Alice starting 14 decimeters from the path and making 6 jumps. The second diagram shows Fred starting 50 decimeters from the path and making 4 jumps in the opposite direction. They both end up at the same place.

b. Explanations will vary. Sample explanation:

If Alice takes four more jumps, she will be at Fred's starting point (50 decimeters from the path).

The four jumps of Fred's in the negative direction were added to Alice's jumps in the positive direction.

Hints and Comments

Overview Students solve equations and describe equations as frog problems.

About the Mathematics In all problems on this page, the starting distance is in the same direction for both frogs, and the jumps are also in the same direction. In other words, the value of x in all of these problems is positive.

Planning Students may work on problem **14** individually.

Comments about the Problems

14. Problems **14** and **15** are similar. They deal with the same situation. You may want to discuss this problem in class, to make sure all students can follow the steps from Box A to Box D. Encourage students to describe their solutions in their own words.

Box C

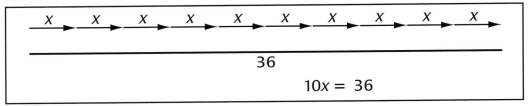

36

$$10x = 36$$

Box D

3.6

$$x = \frac{36}{10} = 3.6$$

15. a. Explain the equation in Box C, and describe how the diagram was changed from Box B to Box C.

   b. Explain the equation in Box D, and describe how the diagram was changed from Box C to Box D.

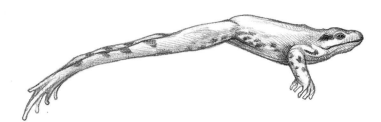

15. a. Explanations will vary. Sample explanation:

Ten jumps are equivalent to 36 decimeters. To get the diagram in Box C, 14 decimeters were subtracted from each length in Box B.

b. Ten jumps is 36 decimeters, so one jump is equal to 36 decimeters ÷ 10 = 3.6 decimeters.

Overview Students solve a frog problem in which two frogs jump toward each other until they meet.

About the Mathematics Students were formally introduced to positive and negative numbers in the grade 6/7 unit *Operations.* In the context of jumps by frogs, the x always stands for the distance. Distance in this context has a direction and a length.

Planning Students may work on problem **15** in small groups.

16. Write a "frog problem" to represent Box A below. You can use Fred and Alice or you may introduce new characters and situations.

Box A

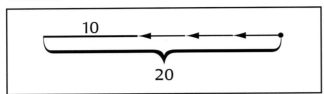

17. a. Draw a diagram to represent the expression $5 + 4x$.

   b. Draw a diagram to represent the expression $12 - 6x$.

18. a. If you start with the equation $27 - 5w = 7 + 3w$, explain why $27 = 7 + 8w$.

   b. Solve the equation.

16. Problems will vary. Sample problem:

A frog starts 20 decimeters from the path and takes three jumps of the same length toward the path. It ends up 10 decimeters from the path.

$20 - 3x = 10$

17. a.

b.

18. a. Explanations will vary. Some students may say that $5w$ has been added to both sides of the equation. Only the 27 remains on the left side, and on the right side $3w$ and $5w$ can be added to make $8w$.

b. $27 - 5w = 7 + 3w$
$27 = 7 + 8w$
$20 = 8w$
$w = 20 \div 8$
$w = 2.5$

Overview Students write another frog problem. They draw diagrams to represent expressions and solve an equation. Then they are introduced to the number line as another model they can use to visualize the frog jumps.

About the Mathematics Number lines have been used in many *Mathematics in Context* units, so students may be familiar with this model. Jumps to the left on the number line are indicated with a minus sign, while jumps to the right are positive. The number line has a dynamic character, because it allows students to draw arrows that represent the moves that are made.

Planning Students may work on problems **16–18** individually.

Comments about the Problems

18. After students have finished problem **18,** you may want to discuss the different kinds of equations students have been solving so far, and how to visualize them using box diagrams. Stress the importance of describing and understanding each step in the solution process.

If students have difficulty expressing what to do to cancel out the $-5w$ on the left side of the equation, you might remind them of the jumps. Tell students that five jumps to the left can be canceled out by five jumps to the right.

Frog problems can also be diagrammed on number lines.

A number line has a positive and negative direction.

Jumps on the number line are considered positive if they move in a positive direction and negative if they move in a negative direction.

For example:

Starting point = −4; jump = +2.5

Starting point = −1; jump = − 3

19. Fred starts at the point −3 and makes 17 jumps in a positive direction. Alice starts at the point 2 and makes 12 jumps in a positive direction. They end at the same point. Assume that every jump is the same length, and use the letter k for that unknown length.

   a. Make up an equation for this situation.

   b. Find the value of k.

   c. Use a number line to check your solution.

20. The equation $8 + 12x = 3 + 2x$ represents a different "frog problem."

   a. Use a number line to explain why the jumps must be in the negative direction.

   b. Solve the equation.

21. Here is an equation for a "frog problem" where the frogs are jumping in opposite directions.

   $$20 + 2v = 26 − 2v$$

   Solve the equation. Then check your answer using a number line.

19. a. $-3 + 17k = 2 + 12k$

b. $k = 1$. Sample strategy:

$$-3 + 17k = 2 + 12k$$
$$-3 + 5k = 2$$
$$5k = 5$$
$$k = 1$$

c.

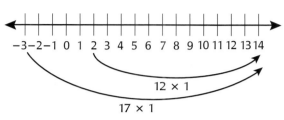

20. a. Answers will vary. Sample response:

The first frog starts at 8 and makes 12 jumps. The second frog starts at 3 and makes 2 jumps. If they both go in a positive direction, the first frog would begin with an advantage of 5 and make 10 more jumps. So it is impossible for the second frog to catch up with the first one.

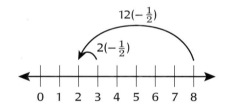

b. $8 + 12x = 3 + 2x$
$8 + 10x = 3$
$10x = -5$
$x = -0.5$

21. $20 + 2v = 26 - 2v$
$20 + 4v = 26$
$4v = 6$
$v = 6 \div 4$
$v = 1.5$

Students may check their answers as follows:

$20 + (2 \times 1.5) = 20 + 3 = 23$
$26 - (2 \times 1.5) = 23$

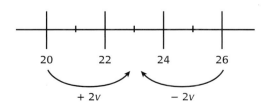

Overview Students solve three frog problems and check their answers using a number line.

About the Mathematics The mathematics in these problems is similar to the mathematics in the problems on page 37 of the Student Book.

Planning Students may work on problems **19–21** individually. These problems can also be assigned as homework or used as informal assessments.

Comments about the Problems

19–21. Homework These problems may be assigned as homework.

19. Informal Assessment This problem assesses students' ability to solve equations of the form $a + bx = c + dx$, and to model a problem situation and translate it to a graph or an equation.

20–21. Informal Assessment These problems assess students' ability to solve equations of the form $a + bx = c + dx$.

Extension You may want to collect some equations from another source, and have students solve them. Have students explain the steps they used to solve each problem.

Writing Opportunity You may ask students to write their answers to problems **19–21** in their notebooks.

In this section, you have solved equations using diagrams and using a number line. Another method is to perform the same operation (addition, subtraction, multiplication, or division) on each side of an equation. Here is an example.

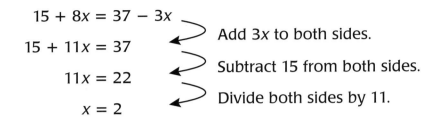

$$15 + 8x = 37 - 3x$$
$$15 + 11x = 37$$ Add $3x$ to both sides.
$$11x = 22$$ Subtract 15 from both sides.
$$x = 2$$ Divide both sides by 11.

22. Study the steps of the example shown above. Use similar steps to complete the solution for the following equation.

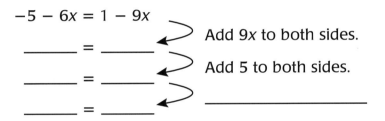

$$-5 - 6x = 1 - 9x$$
_____ = _____   Add $9x$ to both sides.
_____ = _____   Add 5 to both sides.
_____ = _____   _____

23. Here are other steps to solve the same equation as in problem **22.** Complete the solution and check if the result is equal to the result in problem **22.**

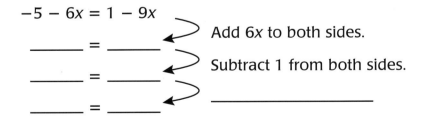

$$-5 - 6x = 1 - 9x$$
_____ = _____   Add $6x$ to both sides.
_____ = _____   Subtract 1 from both sides.
_____ = _____   _____

Solutions and Samples
of student work

22. The completed solution is as follows:

$$-5 - 6x = 1 - 9x$$
$$-5 + 3x = 1$$ Add $9x$ to both sides.
$$3x = 6$$ Add 5 to both sides.
$$x = 2$$ Divide both sides by 3.

23. The completed solution is as follows:

$$-5 - 6x = 1 - 9x$$
$$-5 = 1 - 3x$$ Add $6x$ to both sides.
$$-6 = -3x$$ Subtract 1 from both sides.
$$2 = x$$ Divide both sides by -3.

The value of x in both cases is 2.

Overview Students learn a more formal way to solve equations.

Planning Students may work on problems **22** and **23** individually. Before students work on these problems, you may want to discuss the example at the top of page 39 of the Student Book.

Comments about the Problems

22–23. Make sure that students do not just follow the steps that are given, but also understand and can explain why they should follow these steps.

These problems offer the opportunity to discuss why different methods can produce the same result. You can eliminate the x on the left side of the equation by adding $6x$, or eliminate the x on the right side by adding $9x$. The same method can be used for the starting distances: eliminate them from the right side by subtracting one, or from the left side by adding five.

Summary

In this section, you used frog problems to write and solve equations. You solved equations by drawing diagrams, by using number lines, and by performing an operation (adding, subtracting, multiplying, or dividing) on each side of the equation.

For example, frog A starts 3 decimeters from a log, and frog B starts 5 decimeters from the same log. Frog A and B take jumps that are the same length. Frog A takes 3 jumps and frog B takes 1 jump and meet in the same location, as shown in the diagram below:

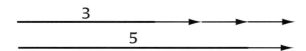

To find out how long the jumps were, you solve the equation for the problem:

$$3 + 3x = 5 + x$$
$$3 + 2x = 5$$
$$2x = 2$$
$$x = 1$$

Summary Questions

24. Solve each equation. You may use any method from this section.

    a. $12 + u = 11 + 3u$

    b. $-4 + 2w = 2 + w$

    c. $10 - v = 24 + v$

25. Write three new "frog problems," one that you think is easy, one that is semi-difficult, and one that is difficult. Describe how to solve each problem.

24. a. $12 + u = 11 + 3u$
$12 = 11 + 2u$
$1 = 2u$
$u = 1 \div 2$
$0.5 = u$

b. $-4 + 2w = 2 + w$
$2w = 6 + w$
$w = 6$

c. $10 - v = 24 + v$
$10 = 24 + 2v$
$-14 = 2v$
$-14 \div 2 = v$
$-7 = v$

25. Problems will vary. Sample problems:

Easy:
$4 + 3x = 7 + 2x$
The frogs both jump in the same direction.

$4 + x = 7$
$x = 3$

Semi-difficult:
$4 + 3x = 19 - 2x$
One frog jumps in a positive direction, and one jumps in a negative direction.

$4 + 5x = 19$
$5x = 15$
$x = 3$

Difficult:
$-4 - 3x = -19 + 2x$
One frog jumps in a positive direction, and one jumps in a negative direction, left of 0.

$-4 = -19 + 5x$
$15 = 5x$
$3 = x$

Overview Students read the Summary, which reviews the main concepts covered in this section.

About the Mathematics It is important that students recognize the different methods for solving equations that they have learned in this section. Students may have a favorite method, but should be able to use other methods as well.

Planning Students may work on problems **24** and **25** individually. These problems can also be used as informal assessments. After students finish Section E, you may assign appropriate activities from the Try This! section, located on pages 45–49 of the *Graphing Equations* Student Book, for homework.

Comments about the Problems

24. Informal Assessment This problem assesses students' ability to solve equations of the form $a + bx = c + dx$ and to choose an appropriate way to solve equations.

This may be a good opportunity for students to share methods and discuss why different methods can still produce the same answer.

25. Informal Assessment This problem assesses students' ability to solve equations of the form $a + bx = c + dx$, and to model a problem situation and translate it to a graph or an equation. It also assesses students' ability to choose an appropriate way to solve equations.

You may want to have students write the three problems, make answer keys for them, and exchange their problems with others in the class. Students can solve and check each other's problems.

Work Students Do

Students locate fires by finding the intersection points of two vision lines. They check the fires' coordinates by solving equations. Students use graphing calculators to graph lines. They see the relationship between parallel lines and graphs of lines without intersection points. Then they relate graphic to algebraic methods of solving equations.

Goals

Students will:

- find and use equations of the form $y = i + sx$ using the slope and y-intercept;

- graph equations of the form $y = i + sx$;

- solve equations of the form $a + bx = c + dx$;

- understand the meaning of slope in different contexts;

- understand how to find the intersection point of two lines, algebraically and graphically;

- understand the graph of a line in the coordinate plane;

- model a problem situation and translate it to a graph or an equation;

- choose an appropriate way to solve equations;

- understand the similarities between graphic and algebraic strategies.

Pacing

- approximately two 45-minute class sessions

Vocabulary

- intersection point

About the Mathematics

A graph of an equation like $y = 3x + 5$ is a representation of all the (x, y) points that are solutions to the equation. Therefore, when two lines are graphed, their point of intersection is the only point that solves both equations. The point of intersection of the two lines shown on the right is $(8, 11)$. This can be determined by combining the equations: $15 - \frac{1}{2}x = -5 + 2x$. Then solve for x, which is 8. Then plug the x value into one of the equations for y: $y = 15 - \frac{1}{2}(8) = 11$.

In this section, students make the connection between the graphic and algebraic methods of solving equations (or finding the point of intersection of two lines).

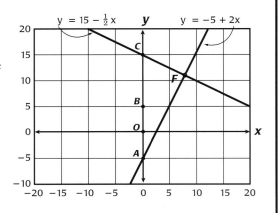

Materials

- graphing calculators, pages 99, 101, 103, and 105 of the Teacher Guide (one per student)
- graph paper, pages 97, 99, 101, and 103 of the Teacher Guide (one sheet per student)

Planning Instruction

You may want to introduce this section by discussing places where lines intersect in real life. Ask students, *What intersecting lines do you see every day?* [Answers will vary, but students might mention street corners, railroad crossings, lines in the structure of furniture or buildings, or lines in nature, such as the lines in spider webs or rock formations.]

Students may work problems 1, 2, 5, and 6 in small groups. They may do the remaining problems individually.

Problem 2 is optional. If you do not have graphing calculators, you may omit it.

Homework

Problems 5 and 6 (page 98 of the Teacher Guide) and 8–11 (page 100 of the Teacher Guide) may be assigned as homework. The Extension activity (page 99 of the Teacher Guide) may also be assigned as homework. After students finish Section F, you may assign appropriate activities from the Try This! section, located on pages 45–49 of the *Graphing Equations* Student Book. The Try This! activities reinforce the key mathematical concepts introduced in this section.

Planning Assessment

- Problems 5 and 6 can be used to informally assess students' ability to graph equations of the form $y = i + sx$, and solve equations of the form $a + bx = c + dx$. They also assess students' ability to understand how to find the intersection point of two lines, algebraically and graphically.

- Problem 8 can be used to informally assess students' ability to understand how to find the intersection point of two lines, algebraically and graphically.

- Problems 11–13 can be used to informally assess students' ability to find and use equations of the form $y = i + sx$ using the slope and y-intercept, and solve equations of the form $a + bx = c + dx$. The problems also assess their ability to understand how to find the intersection point of two lines, algebraically and graphically; to understand the graph of a line in the coordinate plane; to choose an appropriate way to solve equations; and to understand the similarities between graphic and algebraic strategies.

F. INTERSECTING LINES

MEETING ON LINE

Let's return to the park rangers.

Rangers at tower A report a fire on the line whose equation is $y = -5 + 2x$.

Rangers at C report a fire on the line $y = 15 - \frac{1}{2}x$.

The two lines are displayed on a computer screen, as shown on the right.

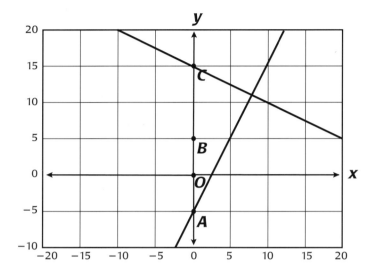

1. **a.** Explain how you can verify that the two lines on the screen represent the two equations.

   b. Using the screen, estimate the coordinates for the fire.

   c. How can you check your coordinates using both equations?

Activity

2. **a.** Using a graphing calculator, show the two lines from towers *A* and *C*.

   b. Use the TRACE function of the calculator to move along one of the two lines. Then jump to the other line. What do you notice about the coordinates of the point as you jump from one line to the other?

   c. What are the coordinates of the fire?

1. **a.** Explanations will vary. One way is to check points on the line. Another is to check the slope and the *y*-intercept.

   b. Estimates will vary, but the *x*-coordinate should be about 8, while the *y*-coordinate should be about 11.

   c. The number chosen for *x* can be substituted into each equation. Both equations should give the same *y* value. For example,

   If $x = 8$, then $y = -5 + (2 \times 8) = 11$, and $y = 15 - (0.5 \times 8) = 11$.

   Therefore, 8 is the *x*-coordinate of the point of intersection for both these equations. The point of intersection is (8, 11).

   If $x = 7$ then $y = -5 + (2 \times 7) = 9$, and $y = 15 - (0.5 \times 7) = 11.5$.

   Since the *x*-coordinate 7 gives the *y*-coordinate 9 in one equation and the *y*-coordinate 11.5 in the other, it can't give the point that fits both equations.

2. **a.** Graphs should look like that pictured on Student Book page 41.

   b. The *x*-coordinate stays the same and the *y*-coordinate changes.

   c. (8, 11)

Materials graphing calculators (one per student); graph paper, optional (one sheet per student)

Overview Students return to the context of park rangers who are locating fires. Students solve equations of lines to find the point of intersection, and they do an activity with a graphing calculator.

About the Mathematics In this section, the relationship between the different representations for solving systems of linear equations is made explicit. Students visualize the point of intersection of two lines on a graphing calculator, use the TRACE feature, solve a linear equation of the form $a + bx = c + dx$, and determine whether a value for *x* gives the same value for *y* in two different equations.

Planning Students may work on problems **1** and **2** in small groups. Problem **2** is optional. If you do not have graphing calculators, you may omit it or have students draw the lines and do the problem using graph paper.

Comments about the Problems

1. Throughout the section, be sure to stress the importance of making a sketch of the graphs, and being able to explain the steps in the process of solving equations. Problem **1c** is critical because students need to understand that the intersection point of two lines is the point that makes both equations true.

   It may be helpful to encourage students to discuss the similarities and differences between the fire problems and the frog problems.

2. To set the window to the right scale, you need the following measures:

x min = −20	*y* min = −10
x max = 20	*y* max = 20
x scl = 5	*y* scl = 5

   On a Texas Instruments graphing calculator, the left and right arrow keys combined with the TRACE key can be used to move along one line. The up and down arrow keys allow users to move between lines. The TRACE feature will not allow students to read an exact value for the location of the fire. You may also want to have students use the INTERSECT or TABLE features on the calculator.

What's the P●int?

Here is another way to find the coordinates of *F*, the *intersection point* of the two lines.

3. Think about the change from points *A* to *F* as a horizontal step followed by a vertical step.

   a. Suppose the length of the horizontal step is represented by *x*. Write an expression for the length of the vertical step.

   b. The change from points *C* to *F* is the same horizontal step *x* followed by a vertical step. Write an expression for the length of that vertical step.

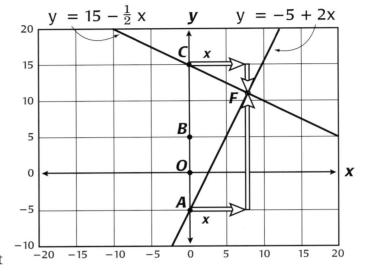

4. From the diagram above, you can set up the following equation:
   $$-5 + 2x = 15 - \tfrac{1}{2}x$$

   a. Write a "frog problem" to go with the equation.

   b. Solve the equation using one of the methods from the previous section.

   c. How can you use your answer from part **b** to find the *y*-coordinate of *F*?

5. The park supervisor has just received two messages:
   Smoke is reported on the line $y = 15 - x$.
   Smoke is reported on the line $y = 5 + 4x$.

   a. Which tower sent each message?

   b. Calculate the coordinates of the smoke.

   c. Check your answer with a graphing calculator.

6. Repeat problem **5** for these two messages:
   Smoke is reported on the line $y = 5 + x$.
   Smoke is reported on the line $y = -5 + 1\tfrac{1}{4}x$.

3. a. The vertical step from point *A* to point *F* is 2*x*, since the slope is equal to 2.

   b. The vertical step from point *C* to point *F* is $-\frac{1}{2}x$, since the slope is equal to $-\frac{1}{2}$.

4. a. Answers will vary. Sample response:

   Alice starts at -5 and takes two jumps of length *x*. Fred starts at 15 and takes a $\frac{1}{2}$ jump of length *x* in the other direction.

   b. *x* = 8. Students may use a variety of strategies to solve this problem. Sample strategy:

   $$-5 + 2x = 15 - \frac{1}{2}x$$
   $$-5 + 2\frac{1}{2}x = 15$$
   $$2\frac{1}{2}x = 20$$
   $$5x = 40$$
   $$x = 40 \div 5$$
   $$x = 8$$

   c. Substitute x = 8 into either of the equations. y = $-5 + 2(8) = 11$. Point *F* is at (8, 11).

5. a. Tower *C* reported smoke on the line $y = 15 - x$. Tower *B* reported smoke on the line $y = 5 + 4x$.

   b. (2, 13). Strategies may vary. Sample strategy:

   $$15 - x = 5 + 4x$$
   $$15 = 5 + 5x$$
   $$10 = 5x$$
   $$10 \div 5 = x$$
   $$x = 2$$
   $$y = 15 - x = 15 - 2 = 13$$

   c. Students graph lines with a calculator and use the TABLE function or the INTERSECT feature to find the coordinates of their intersection.

6. Tower *B* reported smoke on the line $y = 5 + x$. Tower *A* reported smoke on the line $y = -5 + 1\frac{1}{4}x$.

   $$5 + x = -5 + 1\frac{1}{4}x$$
   $$5 = -5 + \frac{1}{4}x$$
   $$10 = \frac{1}{4}x$$
   $$10 \div \frac{1}{4} = x$$
   $$x = 40$$
   $$y = 5 + 40 = 45$$

   The coordinates are (40, 45).

Materials graphing calculators (one per student); graph paper, optional (one sheet per student)

Overview Students solve problems regarding the equation of a line, and solve equations to find the coordinates of the point of intersection of two lines.

About the Mathematics Moves along a line can be described in steps; one step is a move in both the horizontal and the vertical directions. In problem **3,** this graphical way to solve equations is revisited. In problem **4,** the algebraic way (with the frog jumps) is revisited, and in the other problems, any strategy can be used to solve an equation.

Planning Students may work on problems **3** and **4** individually. They may work on problems **5** and **6** in small groups. Problems **5** and **6** can also be assigned as homework or used as informal assessments.

Comments about the Problems

5–6. Informal Assessment These problems assess students' ability to graph equations of the form $y = i + sx$ and to solve equations of the form $a + bx = c + dx$. They also assess students' ability to understand how to find the intersection point of two lines, algebraically and graphically. These problems may also be assigned as homework.

Students may solve these problems using any strategy that they have learned in this unit. If students have difficulty, you might remind them of the strategies they used to solve equations in previous sections. If you have no graphing calculators, you may have students draw the lines on graph paper.

Extension You may want to provide students with more equations, and ask them to draw the corresponding lines and find the points of intersection.

7. The park supervisor received the message $y = 15 + 2x$ from tower C and the message $y = 5 + 3x$ from tower B. What message do you expect from tower A?

8. Make up your own set of messages, and find the location they describe.

9. Suppose the two lines $y = 10 + 2x$ and $y = -8 + 2x$ are on the park rangers' computer screen. What can you tell about these lines? Do they have a point of intersection?

10. Show the two lines $y = -5 + 8x$ and $y = 5 + 7.5x$ on a graphing calculator.

   a. Are the lines parallel? How can you tell for certain?

   b. If the lines are parallel, explain why. If they intersect, find the point of intersection.

11. Look back at the graph for problem **19** on page 21.

   a. Write an equation for each line in the graph.

   b. Use the equations to find the coordinates of the point of intersection.

   c. Compare your answer in part **b** with your answer on page 21.

7. The message from tower A should be $y = -5 + 4x$. Students may use a variety of strategies to solve this problem. Sample strategy:

To find the point where the line from tower B intersects with the line from tower C, make their two equations equal to each other, as follows:

$15 + 2x = 5 + 3x$
$15 = 5 + x$
$x = 10$

When $x = 10$, $y = 5 + 3(10) = 35$.

The point of intersection is at $(10, 35)$.

The line from tower A $(0, -5)$ to $(10, 35)$ has the slope $\frac{40}{10} = 4$. So the line from tower A must be $y = -5 + 4x$.

8. Answers will vary.

9. Both lines have a slope of 2, so they are parallel and will not intersect.

10. a. No. The lines have different slopes.

b. The lines intersect at the point $(20, 155)$. Students may use a variety of strategies to solve this problem. Sample strategy:

$-5 + 8x = 5 + 7.5x$
$-5 + 0.5x = 5$
$0.5x = 10$
$x = 20$

$y = -5 + 8(20)$
$y = -5 + 160$
$y = 155$

The point of intersection is at $(20, 155)$.

11. a. The equation of line ℓ is $y = 3 + \frac{3}{2}x$.

The equation of line m is $y = 2x$.

b. The point of intersection is $(6, 12)$. Strategies will vary. Sample strategy:

$3 + \frac{3}{2}x = 2x$
$3 = \frac{1}{2}x$
$x = 6$

$y = 2(6) = 12$

The point of intersection is at $(6, 12)$.

c. Answers will vary depending on students' previous answers. Hopefully, they are the same.

Materials graphing calculators (one per student); graph paper, optional (one sheet per student)

Overview Students solve a variety of problems about intersecting lines.

About the Mathematics In this unit, students use two major strategies to solve equations of the kind $ax + b = cx + d$. The first makes use of the graphs, and the second is the algebraic way dealt with in Section E. Students should be able to use both methods.

Planning Students may work on problems **7–11** individually. Problems **8–11** may be assigned as homework. Problems **8** and **11** may also be used as informal assessments.

Comments about the Problems

8–11. Homework These problems may be assigned as homework. While students solve these problems, encourage them to draw the lines that are described by the equations.

8. Informal Assessment This problem can be used to assess students' ability to understand how to find the intersection point of two lines, algebraically and graphically.

11. Informal Assessment This problem assesses students' ability to find and use equations of the form $y = i + sx$ using the slope and y-intercept, and solve equations of the form $a + bx = c + dx$. It also assesses their ability to understand how to find the intersection point of two lines, algebraically and graphically. Finally, it assesses students' ability to understand the graph of a line in the coordinate plane, choose an appropriate way to solve equations, and understand the similarities between graphic and algebraic strategies.

Summary

An equation for line ℓ is $y = 1 + 3x$, and the equation for line m is $y = -3 - 2x$.

You can find the intersection point of these two lines by solving the following equation for x:

$-3 - 2x = 1 + 3x$.

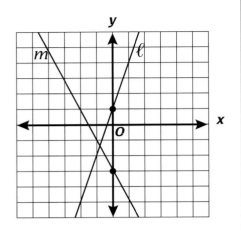

Summary Questions

12. **a.** Find the x-value of the intersection of the lines shown above by solving the equation $-3 - 2x = 1 + 3x$.

b. Find the y-value of the point of intersection of lines j and k shown on the graph below.

c. Check your answers to parts **a** and **b** using a graphing calculator.

13. Write an equation for each line shown in the graph on the right. Then use the equations to find the intersection of the two lines.

14. Refer to problem **17** on page 27. Use the intercept function of a graphing calculator to find the points of intersection of the lines.

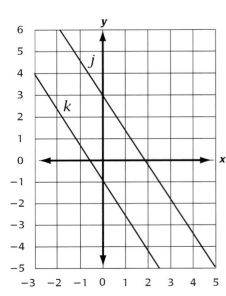

12. a. At the point of intersection, $x = -\frac{4}{5}$.

$$-3 - 2x = 1 + 3x$$
$$-3 = 1 + 5x$$
$$-4 = 5x$$
$$x = -\frac{4}{5}$$

b. At the point of intersection $y = -\frac{7}{5}$.

$$y = 1 + 3(-\frac{4}{5})$$
$$y = \frac{5}{5} + -\frac{12}{5} = -\frac{7}{5}$$

Note: On Student Book page 44, have students change the references in this problem. The problem should refer to lines ℓ and m on the graph *above*.

c. Students should use graphing calculators to verify the point of intersection as $(-\frac{4}{5}, -\frac{7}{5})$

13. The equation of line j is $y = 3 - \frac{8}{5}x$.

The equation of line k is $y = -1 - \frac{5}{3}x$.

The point of intersection is $(-60, 99)$. Sample strategy:

$$3 - \frac{8}{5}x = -1 - \frac{5}{3}x \qquad \text{add } \frac{8}{5} x \text{ to both sides}$$
$$3 = -1 + (\frac{8}{5} - \frac{5}{3})x \qquad \text{add 1 to both sides}$$
$$4 = -\frac{1}{15}x \qquad \text{multiply to both sides by } -15$$

$$x = -60$$

$$y = 3 - \frac{8}{5}(-60)$$
$$y = 3 - (-96) = 99$$

14.

Lines	Approximate Intersection Points
1 and 2	(15, 20)
1 and 4	(0, 15)
1 and 5	(30, 25)
1 and 6	(−6.25, 13.75)
2 and 3	(0, 5)
2 and 4	(2.75, 7.5)
2 and 6	(−2.5, 2.5)
3 and 4	(3, 1)
3 and 6	(−3, −1)
4 and 5	(5, 0)
5 and 6	(0, −5)

Materials graphing calculators (one per student); graph paper, optional (one sheet per student)

Overview Students read the Summary, which reviews the main concepts covered in this section. Students solve problems about equations of lines, and find the points of intersection of lines.

About the Mathematics Students may use several strategies for finding the point of intersection of two lines. It is important that they understand the concepts and procedures that play a role. Students should be able to solve these kinds of problems using paper and pencil.

Planning Students may work on problems **12–14** individually. Problems **12** and **13** can also be used as informal assessments. After students finish Section F, you may assign appropriate activities from the Try This! section, located on pages 45–49 of the *Graphing Equations* Student Book, for homework.

Comments about the Problems

12–13. Informal Assessment These problems assess students' ability to find and use equations of the form $y = i + sx$ using the slope and y-intercept, to graph equations of the form $y = i + sx$, and to solve equations of the form $a + bx = c + dx$. They also assess students' ability to understand how to find the intersection point of two lines, algebraically and graphically. Finally, they assess students' ability to understand the graph of a line in the coordinate plane, to model a problem situation and translate it to a graph or an equation, to choose an appropriate way to solve equations, and to understand the similarities between graphic and algebraic strategies.

14. The following directions will help if you use the CALC Intersect feature of a Texas Instruments calculator to find the intersection of line 1 and line 6, stored in Y1 and Y6 respectively.

After you select 5:INTERSECT from the CALC menu, the Y1 equation will be in the upper left-hand corner. Press ENTER for the first curve. Equation Y6 is in the upper left-hand corner. Press ENTER. Pressing ENTER again will display the point of intersection.

Students work on two assessment activities that you can use to collect additional information about what each student knows about describing lines, solving equations, and graphing equations.

Goals

- describe and graph directions using wind directions and angles

- use inequalities to describe regions restricted by vertical and horizontal lines

- find and use equations of the form $y = i + sx$ using the slope and y-intercept

- graph equations of the form $y = i + sx$

- solve equations of the form $a + bx = c + dx$

- understand the meaning of slope in different contexts

- understand how to find the intersection point of two lines, algebraically and graphically

- understand the graph of a line in the coordinate plane

- model a problem situation and translate it to a graph or an equation

- choose an appropriate way to solve equations

- understand the similarities between graphic and algebraic strategies

Assessment Problems

Treasure Island

Treasure Island

Rent a Car
Treasure Island

Rent a Car
Treasure Island

Rent a Car
Treasure Island

Treasure Island

Rent a Car
Treasure Island

Rent a Car
Treasure Island

Rent a Car

Treasure Island

Rent a Car

Pacing

When combined, the two assessment activities will take approximately two or three 45-minute class sessions. For more information on how to use the two problems, see the Planning Assessment section on the next page.

About the Mathematics

The two assessment activities evaluate the major goals of the *Graphing Equations* unit. Refer to the Goals and Assessment Opportunities sections on the previous page for information regarding the specific goals assessed in each assessment activity. Students may use different strategies to solve each problem. Their choice of strategies may indicate their level of comprehension of the problem. Consider how well students' strategies address the problem, as well as how successful students are at applying their strategies in the problem-solving process.

Materials

- Assessments, pages 121–123 of the Teacher Guide (one of each per student)
- graph paper, page 107 of the Teacher Guide (one sheet per student)
- graphing calculators, page 107 of the Teacher Guide, optional (one per student)

Planning Assessment

You may want students to work on these assessments individually so that you can evaluate each student's understanding and abilities. Make sure that you allow enough time for students to complete the assessment activities. Students are free to solve each problem in their own way. They may choose to use any of the models introduced and developed in this unit to solve problems that do not call for a specific model.

You might want to use the Rent a Car assessment any time after students finish Section E, and the Treasure Island assessment any time after students finish Section F.

Scoring

Answers are provided for all assessment problems. The method of scoring the problems depends on the types of questions in each assessment. Most questions require students to explain their reasoning or justify their answers. For these questions, the reasoning used by the students in solving the problems as well as the correctness of the answers should be considered as part of your grading scheme. A holistic scoring scheme can be used to evaluate an entire task. For example, after reviewing a student's work, you may assign a key word such as *emerging, developing, accomplishing,* or *exceeding* to describe his or her mathematical problem-solving, reasoning, and communication.

On other tasks, it may be more appropriate to assign point values for each response. Student progress toward the goals of the unit should also be considered. Descriptive statements that include details of a student's solution to an assessment activity can be recorded. These statements could provide insight into a student's progress toward a specific goal of the unit. Descriptive statements are often more informative than recording only a score and can be used to document student growth in mathematics over time.

RENT A CAR

Use additional paper as needed.

A man from Nigeria visits the United States and wants to rent a car. He gets information about the prices of car rentals from two companies. Here are the two possibilities:

ARRIVE RENTAL CAR
$40/day
plus $0.25 per km

Best Rental Car
$50 a day
and only
$0.21 a km

1. Suppose the man plans to drive 200 kilometers in one day. Which of the two companies has the less expensive rate?

2. Which of the two companies is less expensive if he plans to drive 300 kilometers in one day?

The formula to calculate the price for the Arrive Rental Car Company is as follows:
price $= 40 + 0.25d$

3. Explain this formula.

4. Write a formula for the Best Rental Car Company.

5. Is there any distance for which both companies have equal rates?
(Solve this problem by using an equation.)

6. Make a graph to illustrate the relationship between distance and price for Arrive and Best.

7. How can you find the answer to problem **5** in the diagram?

8. For what distances is Arrive cheaper? For what distances is Best cheaper?

1. Arrive Rental Car offers the less expensive rate.

At Arrive, a car costs $90.
$40 + \$0.25 \times 200 = \$90.00$

At Best, a car costs $92.
$50 + \$0.21 \times 200 = \$92.00$

2. A rental car from Best costs less for a 300-km trip.

At Arrive, a car costs $115.
$40 + 0.25 \times 300 = \$115.00$

At Best, a car costs $113.00.
$50 + 0.21 \times 300 = \$113.00$

3. The number 40 represents the initial cost everyone must pay. The cost per kilometer is $0.25, and d is the distance in kilometers a customer plans to drive.

4. price $= 50 + 0.21d$

5. Yes. They have equal rates for a 250-kilometer trip.
$40 + 0.25d = 50 + 0.21d$
$40 + 0.04d = 50$
$0.04d = 10$
$d = \frac{10}{0.04} = 250$

6.

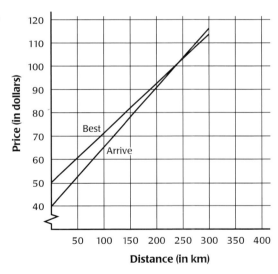

7. It is the intersection point of the two lines.

8. If a customer plans to drive less than 250 km, it is cheaper to rent a car at Arrive. If a customer plans to drive more than 250 km, it is cheaper to rent a car at Best. At a distance of 250 km, both rental companies charge the same amount ($102.50).

Materials graph paper (one sheet per student); graphing calculators, optional (one per student)

Overview Students determine which of two car rental companies is cheaper, depending on how far a customer plans to drive.

About the Mathematics These activities assess students' ability to find and use equations of the form $y = i + sx$ using the slope and y-intercept, graph equations of the form $y = i + sx$, and solve equations of the form $a + bx = c + dx$. They also assess students' ability to find the intersection point of two lines, algebraically and graphically. Finally, these activities assess students' ability to understand the graph of a line in the coordinate plane, model a problem situation and translate it to a graph or an equation, and understand the similarities between graphic and algebraic strategies.

Planning You may want students to work on these assessment problems individually.

Comments about the Problems

1–8. The TABLE feature of a graphing calculator can be a useful tool for solving and explaining solutions to this page.

3. Students should be able to interpret and explain the formula in terms of slope and y-intercept.

5. Students should recognize that they must either find the point of intersection (using a graphical solution) or solve the equation (using an algebraic solution).

7. In this problem, students should show an understanding of the relationship between the graphic and algebraic methods.

8. You may want to ask students to show inequality signs in their answers.

Use additional paper as needed.

From April 1760 until September 1763, Captain Peter Robertson made many voyages filled with strange adventures. One day he found a large box of precious jewels. Frightened by pirates, he decided to hide the treasure on a deserted Pacific island. A few weeks after he returned home to London, he fell ill and died. He was only 43 years old. On his deathbed, he gave a map of the island to his two children.

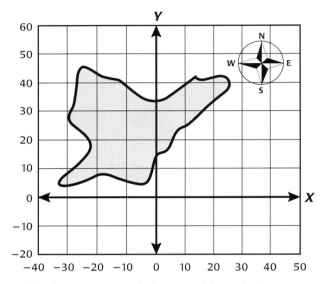

The treasure is buried near a big palm tree, on a spot of which I know:
North equals the year of my departure plus 4 times West.
Also: North equals two times East plus the year of my birth.

The two children, Lawrence and Mary, puzzled over the map. After some time, Lawrence said, "North means north-coordinate." Later, Mary said, "The year of Father's departure was 1760, but probably he meant 60."

So they wrote two equations based on their father's will.

1. The first equation is $y = 60 - 4x$. Explain how Mary found this equation.

2. Write the second equation with y and x. Explain your equation.

3. Draw lines on the map to determine where the treasure is buried.

4. Calculate both coordinates of this place by solving the equations.

1. Explanations will vary. Sample explanation:

North is represented by y and south by $-y$. East is represented by x and west by $-x$. Captain Robertson's departure is at north = 60 plus 4 times west. Using the y and x for the directions, you get the following equation: $y = 60 - 4x$

2. $y = 2x + 20$. Explanations will vary. Sample explanation:

North = 20 + 2 times east, where 20 is the year of Captain Robertson's birth; $y = 2x + 20$ or $y = 20 + 2x$

3.

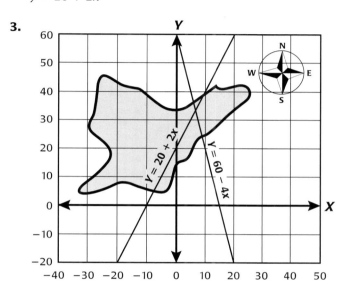

4. $(6\frac{2}{3}, 33\frac{1}{3})$. Sample strategy:

Setting the two equations equal to one another and solving first for x:

$60 - 4x = 2x + 20$
$40 = 6x$
$6\frac{2}{3} = x$

$x = \frac{20}{3}$
$y = 60 - 4 \times \frac{20}{3}$
$y = 60 - \frac{80}{3}$
$y = \frac{(180 - 80)}{3} = \frac{100}{3}$
$y = 33\frac{1}{3}$

Overview Students use equations (and their corresponding graphs) to find the location of a treasure on an island.

About the Mathematics These activities assess students' ability to describe and graph directions using wind directions and angles, to use inequalities to describe regions restricted by horizontal and vertical lines, and to find and use equations of the form $y = i + sx$ using the slope and y-intercept. These activities also evaluate their ability to graph equations of the form $y = i + sx$, solve equations of the form $a + bx = c + dx$, and understand the meaning of slope in different contexts. Finally, these activities evaluate students' ability to understand how to find the intersection point of two lines, algebraically and graphically; to understand the graph of a line in the coordinate plane; and to choose an appropriate way to solve equations.

Planning You may want students to work on these assessment problems individually.

Comments about the Problems

1. Students should demonstrate that they understand how to find this equation.

2. Students may write the equation using east-west and north-south or x and y.

3. When students draw the lines, it will be hard to read the coordinates of the point of intersection.

4. Students should realize that they can use an equation to find exact coordinates, something that is not possible using only the graph.

Use additional paper as needed.

Lawrence and Mary made a voyage to Treasure Island. The wind was favorable, and they reached the island in seven weeks.

5. Lawrence and Mary arrived at the northernmost point on the island. Estimate the coordinates of that point.

When they walked in the direction of the buried treasure, they came to a large marsh. The region of the marsh can be described by the following inequalities:

$$-20 < x < -10 \text{ and } 20 < y < 40$$

Lawrence and Mary walked south of the marsh, and then took the shortest route to the treasure spot.

6. On the map, draw a possible route from the point of arrival to the treasure spot.

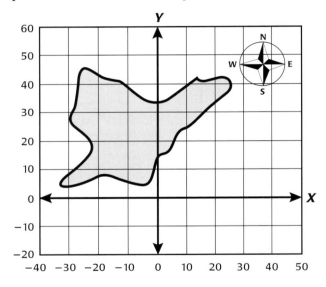

They found the place where they had to dig, and they dug until they found a little box. Inside the box they did not find the treasure, but instead found a letter:

The real spot where I buried the treasure is not far from here. Of the two equations described on the map, only one is valid. The other equation you need is:
$$y = 40 - 2x$$
Good luck!

7. Decide which of the equations from the first letter is valid and determine the coordinates of the spot where Lawrence and Mary have to dig. Use the map and write down your calculations and your line of reasoning.

5. (−25, 45)

6. Routes will vary. Sample route:

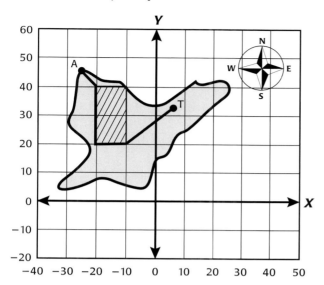

7. The valid equations are $y = 40 - 2x$ and $y = 20 + 2x$. Lawrence and Mary should dig at the spot (5, 30). Explanations will vary. Sample explanation:

The equation, $y = 60 - 4x$ is not valid. The point of intersection for $y = 40 - 2x$ and $y = 60 - 4x$ does not fall on the island, but out at sea.

$y = 40 - 2x$ and $y = 20 + 2x$

$40 - 2x = 20 + 2x$
$20 = 4x$
$5 = x$

$y = 40 - 2 \times 5$
$y = 30$

Overview Students continue to investigate the location of the treasure and use inequalities to indicate a region.

About the Mathematics These assessment problems evaluate students' ability to describe and graph directions using wind directions and angles, to use inequalities to describe regions restricted by horizontal and vertical lines, and to find and use equations of the form $y = i + sx$ using the slope and y-intercept. These activities also evaluate students' ability to graph equations of the form $y = i + sx$, to solve equations of the form $a + bx = c + dx$, and to understand the meaning of slope in different contexts. Finally, these activities evaluate students' ability to understand how to find the intersection point of two lines, algebraically and graphically; to understand the graph of a line in the coordinate plane; and to choose an appropriate way to solve equations.

Planning You may want students to work on these assessment problems individually.

Comments about the Problems

5. Students should show that they can estimate the coordinates of a point on the map that is not determined by intersecting lines of the grid.

6. There are many possible routes. The problem does not ask for the shortest route, so students can draw any route. The problem does not even ask for a route with straight lines. You may want to make the problem more closed by adding the following restrictions: students should draw the route that is shortest and that uses straight lines.

7. This problem is more difficult than the previous ones. Students are asked to write about their thinking process.

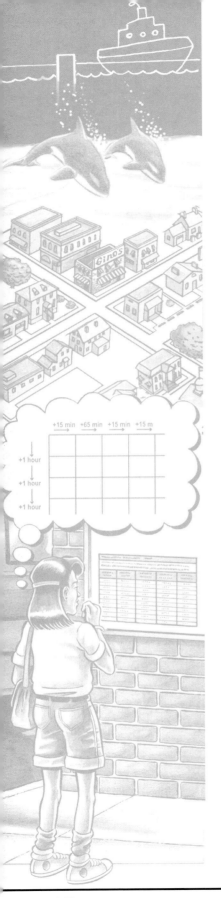

Graphing Equations
Glossary

The Glossary defines all vocabulary words listed on the Section Opener pages. It includes the mathematical terms that may be new to students, as well as words having to do with the contexts introduced in the unit. (Note: The Student Book has no glossary. This is in order to allow students to construct their own definitions, based on their personal experiences with the unit activities.)

The definitions below are specific to the use of the terms in this unit. The page numbers given are from this Teacher Guide.

< and > signs (p. 32) inequality symbols that represent the relations less than (<) and greater than (>)

compass rose (p. 8) a circle that shows the four main directions (north, east, south, and west) and the in-between directions (northeast, southeast, southwest, and northwest)

coordinate system (p. 26) a rectangular grid used as a means for locating points in a plane; such a system has two number lines (called axes) placed at right angles to one another, which intersect at a point called the origin

degree measurements (p. 10) directions as measured in degrees; a circle has 360° (north can be placed at 0 degrees and measurements can be taken clockwise, or the positive x-axis can be 0 degrees and measurements can be taken counterclockwise)

equation (p. 30) a formula expressed as an equivalency ($y = 3$)

equation of a line (p. 62) an equation such as $y = i + sx$ that when graphed is a line

horizontal line (p. 30) a fixed line in a coordinate system parallel to the x-axis

horizontal component (p. 48) the distance in the horizontal direction that is used to measure the slope of a line

intercept (p. 62) the point at which a graph intersects the x- or y-axis

intersection point (p. 98) the point at which two lines meet

origin (p. 26) the point where the x- and y-axes intersect in a coordinate system

quadrant (p. 26) one of four parts of a coordinate system as defined by the x- and y-axes

slope (p. 48) a measure of the steepness and direction of a line; the slope can be found by using two points on the line; it is the ratio of the vertical distance between the two points divided by the horizontal distance between the same two points

tangent (p. 68) a measure of the steepness of a line; the tangent of the angle that a line makes with the right side of the x-axis is the slope of the line

unknown (p. 78) a number that is not known, which is usually represented by a letter or a symbol in an equation or inequality

vertical line (p. 30) a fixed line in a coordinate system parallel to the y-axis

vertical component (p. 48) the distance in the vertical direction that is used to measure the slope of a line

x-axis (p. 26) the horizontal axis in a rectangular coordinate system

x-coordinate (p. 28) a number that designates the distance along the horizontal axis

y-axis (p. 26) the vertical axis in a coordinate system

y-coordinate (p. 28) a number that designates the distance along the vertical axis

Mathematics
in
Context

Blackline
Masters

Dear Family,

Your child will soon begin the *Mathematics In Context* unit *Graphing Equations.* Below is a letter to your child that opens the unit, describing the unit and its goals.

Your child will look at the way forest fires are reported from two lookout towers. This leads to a number of different ways of describing the location of the fire. Your child will describe the locations of fires, first informally, based on directions, and then formally, using equations in a coordinate plane. In the context of a realistic situation involving a fire, your child will solve some complex mathematical equations. You might ask your child to share what he or she is learning about locating fires.

In this unit, your child will use a graphing calculator as a tool to graph lines and find an equation for a drawn line. Algebra will be connected to geometry as the angle and its tangent ratio are used to build your child's understanding of the concept of slope.

Toward the end of the unit, you might ask your child how he or she can find the intersection of one or more lines by using graphs and solving equations.

Enjoy helping your child to explore linear equations.

Sincerely,

The Mathematics in Context Development Team

Dear Student,

You will soon begin the unit *Graphing Equations.* The focus of this unit is the study of lines. At first you will investigate how forest fires can be reported by park rangers at observation towers. You will learn many different ways to describe directions, lines, and locations. As you do, keep an eye out for other uses of lines and coordinates in your day-to-day activities.

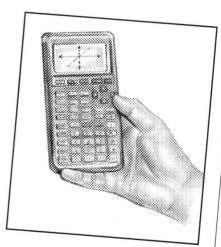

As part of this unit, you will use a graphing calculator to explore several ways to find the point of intersection of two lines. After you complete this unit, you will be able to use a graphing calculator to discover many more features of lines, points, coordinates, and equations.

We hope you will enjoy this unit.

Sincerely,

The Mathematics in Context Development Team

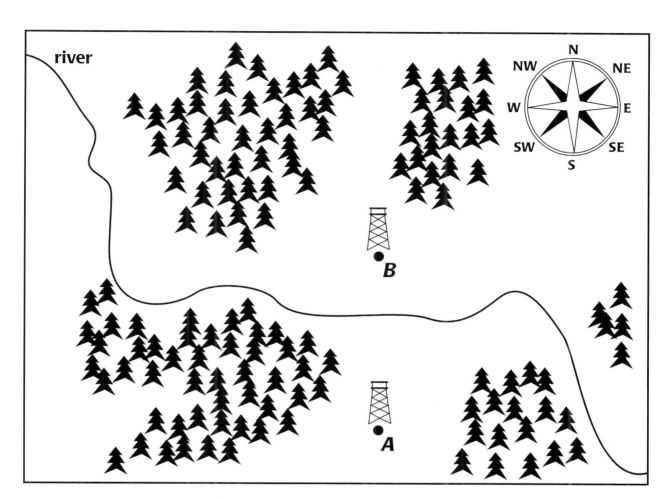

Use with *Graphing Equations,* page 4.

5. Smoke is reported at 8° from tower *A,* and the same smoke is reported at 26° from tower *B.* Use this sheet to show the exact location of the fire.

6. Use this sheet to show the exact location of a fire if rangers report smoke at 342° from tower *A* and 315° from tower *B.*

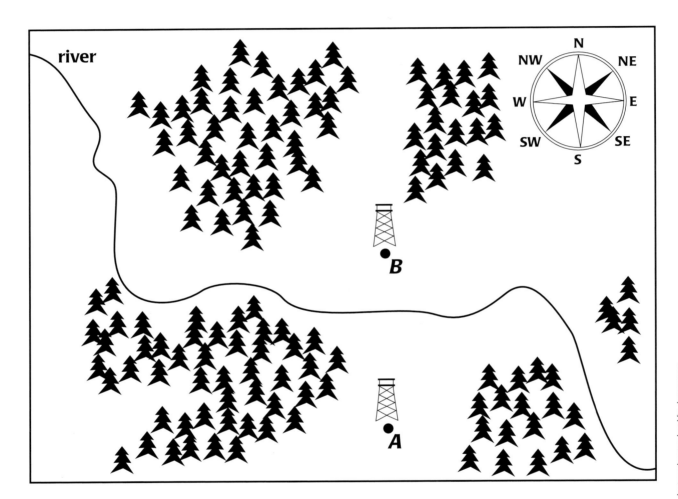

7. The firefighters receive reports of smoke that is 294° from tower *A*, 247° from tower *B*, and 210° from tower *C*.

   a. The firefighters know that something is wrong with these reports. Explain how they know.

   b. Further reports confirm that the observations from towers *A* and *C* are correct but the observation from tower *B* is incorrect. Find the correct observation to report from tower *B*.

8. On another day, rangers report smoke at a direction of 240° from tower *A and* from tower *B*. Is it possible that both reports are correct? Why or why not?

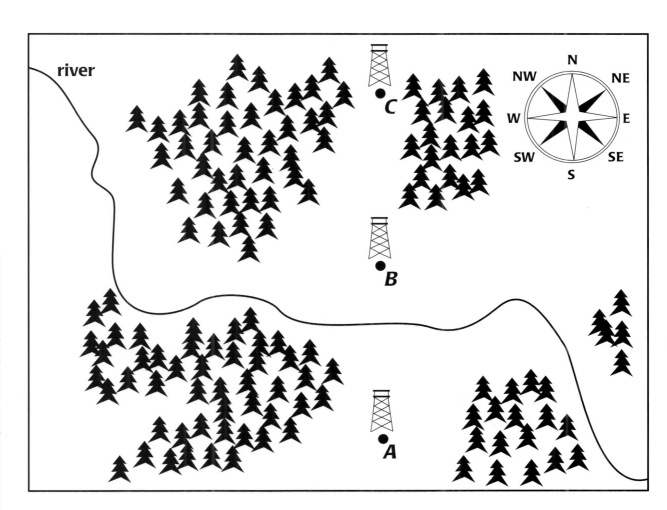

Use with *Graphing Equations,* pages 12 and 13.

13. There are firebreaks that follow parts of the lines described by the equations $x = 14$, $x = 16$, $x = 18$, $y = 8$, $y = 6$, $y = 4$, $y = 2$, and $y = 0$.

   a. Draw the firebreaks through the wooded regions of the park on the graph below.

   b. Which of these firebreaks is the longest? Approximately how long is it?

14. Show the restricted region for a fire that starts at the point (17, 5).

15. Another fire starts at the point (15, 3). The fire is restricted to a region by four firebreaks. Show the region on the graph and describe it.

16. Use this graph and a pencil of a different color to show the region described by the inequalities $-6 < x < -3$ and $6 < y < 10$.

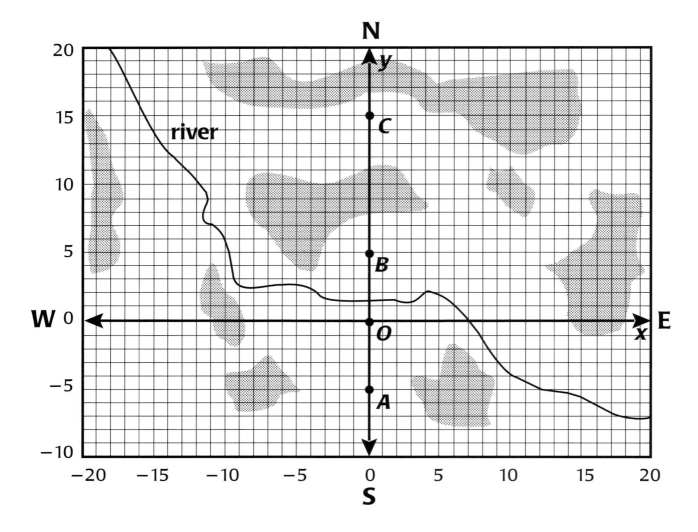

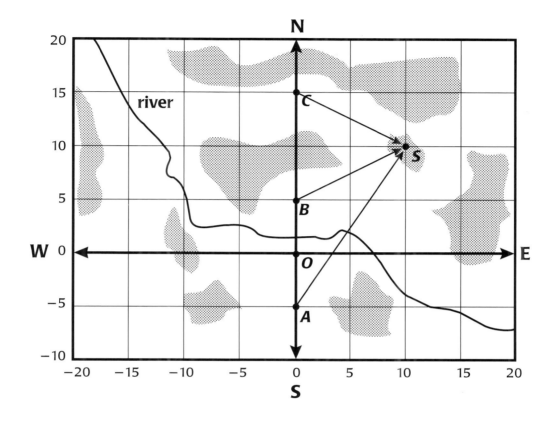

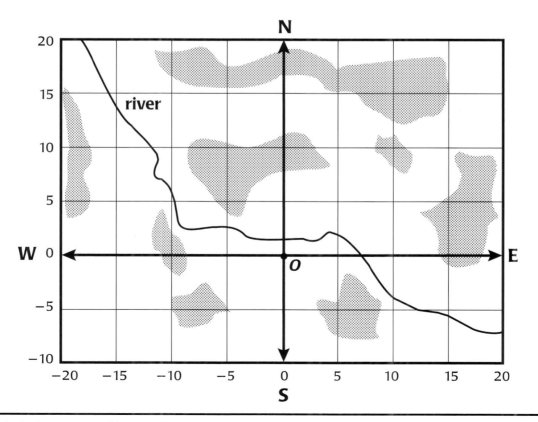

Name _____

Use with *Graphing Equations,* page 20.

16. Each of the lines below contain the point (0, 0). For some of the lines, the slope is labeled inside its circle. Fill in the empty circles with the correct slope.

17. What do you know about two lines that contain the same slope?

18. Draw and label the line through (0, 0) whose slope is:

   a. $\frac{4}{3}$

   b. $-\frac{1}{2}$

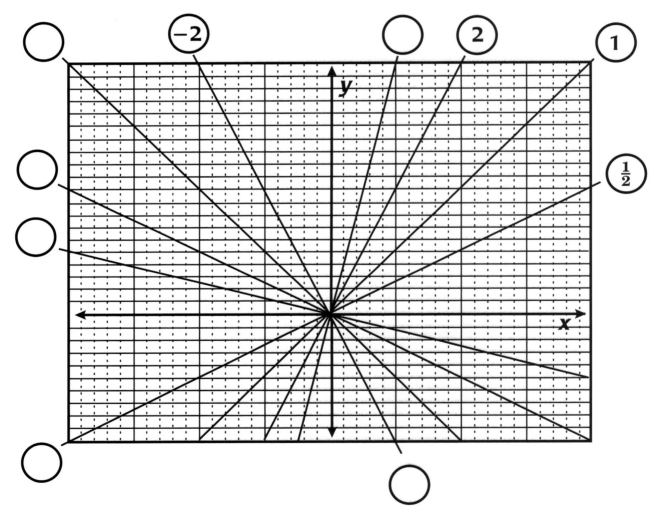

RENT A CAR

Use additional paper as needed.

A man from Nigeria visits the United States and wants to rent a car. He gets information about the prices of car rentals from two companies. Here are the two possibilities:

ARRIVE RENTAL CAR
$40/day
plus $0.25 per km

Best Rental Car
$50 a day
and only
$0.21 a km

1. Suppose the man plans to drive 200 kilometers in one day. Which of the two companies has the less expensive rate?

2. Which of the two companies is less expensive if he plans to drive 300 kilometers in one day?

The formula to calculate the price for the Arrive Rental Car Company is as follows:
price = 40 + 0.25d

3. Explain this formula.

4. Write a formula for the Best Rental Car Company.

5. Is there any distance for which both companies have equal rates?
(Solve this problem by using an equation.)

6. Make a graph to illustrate the relationship between distance and price for Arrive and Best.

7. How can you find the answer to problem **5** in the diagram?

8. For what distances is Arrive cheaper? For what distances is Best cheaper?

Use additional paper as needed.

From April 1760 until September 1763, Captain Peter Robertson made many voyages filled with strange adventures. One day he found a large box of precious jewels. Frightened by pirates, he decided to hide the treasure on a deserted Pacific island. A few weeks after he returned home to London, he fell ill and died. He was only 43 years old. On his deathbed, he gave a map of the island to his two children.

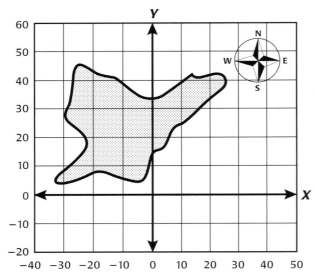

The treasure is buried near a big palm tree, on a spot of which I know:
North equals the year of my departure plus 4 times West.
Also: North equals two times East plus the year of my birth.

The two children, Lawrence and Mary, puzzled over the map. After some time, Lawrence said, "North means north-coordinate." Later, Mary said, "The year of Father's departure was 1760, but probably he meant 60."

So they wrote two equations based on their father's will.

1. The first equation is $y = 60 - 4x$. Explain how Mary found this equation.

2. Write the second equation with y and x. Explain your equation.

3. Draw lines on the map to determine where the treasure is buried.

4. Calculate both coordinates of this place by solving the equations.

Use additional paper as needed.

Lawrence and Mary made a voyage to Treasure Island. The wind was favorable, and they reached the island in seven weeks.

5. Lawrence and Mary arrived at the northernmost point on the island. Estimate the coordinates of that point.

When they walked in the direction of the buried treasure, they came to a large marsh. The region of the marsh can be described by the following inequalities:

$$-20 < x < -10 \text{ and } 20 < y < 40$$

Lawrence and Mary walked south of the marsh, and then took the shortest route to the treasure spot.

6. On the map, draw a possible route from the point of arrival to the treasure spot.

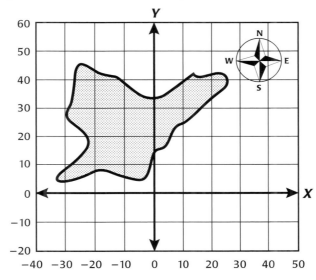

They found the place where they had to dig, and they dug until they found a little box. Inside the box they did not find the treasure, but instead found a letter:

The real spot where I buried the treasure is not far from here. Of the two equations described on the map, only one is valid. The other equation you need is:
$$y = 40 - 2x$$
Good luck!

7. Decide which of the equations from the first letter is valid and determine the coordinates of the spot where Lawrence and Mary have to dig. Use the map and write down your calculations and your line of reasoning.

Section A. Forest Fire

1. approximately 38°

2. The opposite direction is 155°. Hayward airport is in that direction.

3. The skyscraper is about 1 kilometer west of the San Francisco–Oakland Bay Bridge. See map on the right.

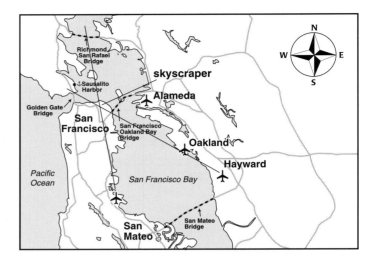

Section B. Coordinates on a Screen

1. The coordinates of Oakland airport are (7, 4).

2. The equation is $x = -4$.

3. See the graph below.

4. The region is described by the inequalities $5 < x < 10$ and $-3 < y < 0$

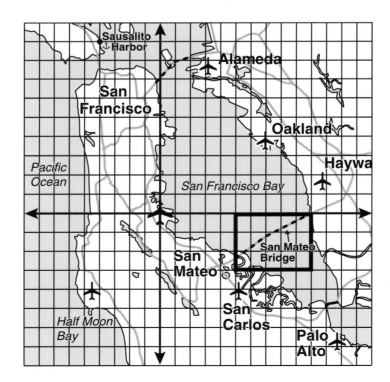

Section C. Directions as Pairs of Numbers

1. *P* is in the direction [−4, 8].

2.

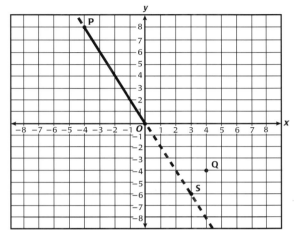

3. No, *Q* is in the direction [4, −4]; that is different from [−4, 8].

4. Yes, *S* is on the same line, but in the opposite direction from *O*. See the graph above.

5. From *P* to *Q*, you go 12 units down and 8 to the right, so the slope is $-\frac{12}{8}$ or $-\frac{3}{2}$.

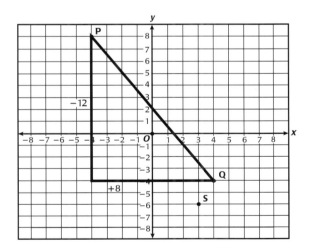

Section D. An Equation of a Line

1.   **a.**   Graphs will vary. Sample graph.

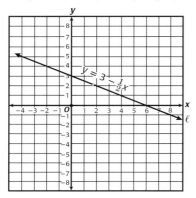

   b.   Graphs will vary.

   For line graphed above, the equation is $y = 3 - \frac{1}{2}x$.

2. a–b.   Graphs will vary. Sample graphs.

   For the lines graphed above, the slope of the line intersecting line m is equal to $-\frac{1}{4}$, and its y-intercept is (0, 3). The two lines intersect at (8, 1).

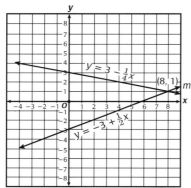

3. a–b.

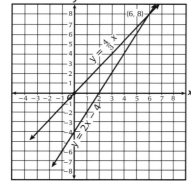

   The equation for the line through points (0, 0) and (6, 8) is $y = \frac{4}{3}x$. The y-intercept is (0, 0). The slope is equal to $\frac{8}{6}$ or $\frac{4}{3}$. So, the equation is $y = \frac{4}{3}x$.

Section E. Solving Equations

1. a. $12 + 2x = 5 + 4x$

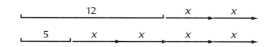

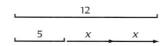

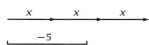

x = 3.5

b. $-5 + 3x = 16 - 4x$

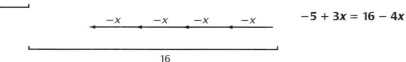

−5 + 3x = 16 − 4x

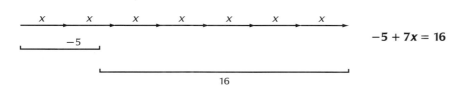

−5 + 7x = 16

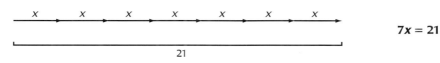

7x = 21

x = 3

2. a. Story problems will vary. Sample story problem:

Frog A starts at a distance of 4 and makes 3 jumps to the right
Frog B starts at a distance of 19 and makes 2 jumps to the right the length of the jump *x* is 15.

$4 + 3x = 19 + 2x$
$4 + x = 19$
$x = 15$

b. Story problems will vary. Sample story problem:

One frog starts at a distance 4 left of zero and makes 3 jumps to the right. The other frog starts at 19 left of zero and makes two jumps to the right. The length of the jump *x* is −15.

$-4 + 3x = -19 + 2x$
$-4 + x = -19$
$x = -15$

Section F. Intersecting Lines

1. line ℓ, since it has a positive slope and the y-intercept is 1.5

2. Line m has the equation $y = 3 - \frac{4}{6}x$ or $y = 3 - \frac{2}{3}x$.

3. $\left(\frac{18}{11}, \frac{21}{11}\right)$

$\frac{3}{2} + \frac{1}{4}x = 3 - \frac{2}{3}x$

$\frac{3}{2} + \frac{3}{12}x = 3 - \frac{8}{12}x$

$\frac{3}{12}x + \frac{8}{12}x = 3 - \frac{3}{2}$

$\frac{11}{12}x = \frac{3}{2}$

$x = \frac{3}{2} \times \frac{12}{11}$

$x = \frac{18}{11}$

if $x = \frac{18}{11}$, $y = \frac{3}{2} + \frac{1}{4}\left(\frac{18}{11}\right)$

$y = \frac{3}{2} + \frac{9}{22}$

$y = \frac{33}{22} + \frac{9}{22}$

$y = \frac{42}{22}$

$y = \frac{21}{11}$

The point of intersection is $\left(\frac{18}{11}, \frac{21}{11}\right)$.

4. The equation of line p is $y = -1 + \frac{2}{3}x$.

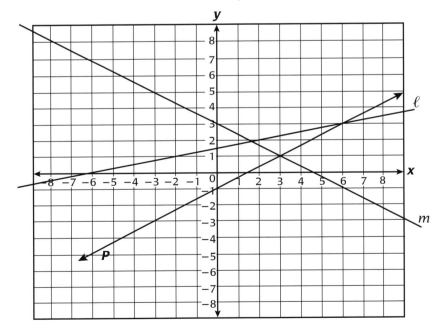

5. Check the display windows of students' graphing calculators.

Cover

Design by Ralph Paquet/Encyclopædia Britannica Educational Corporation.

Collage by Koorosh Jamalpur/KJ Graphics.

Title Page

Illustration by Patricia Parra/Navta Associates, Inc.

Illustrations

3, 6 Meryl Treatner/Navta Associates, Inc.; **8** Ann Barrow/Navta Associates, Inc.; **10, 12, 14, 20** Meryl Treatner/Navta Associates, Inc.; **22, 24, 26** Ann Barrow/Navta Associates, Inc.; **30, 38, 44, 48, 58** Meryl Treatner/Navta Associates, Inc.; **60** Ann Barrow/Navta Associates, Inc.; **64, 66** Meryl Treatner/Navta Associates, Inc.; **74, 76, 78, 80, 82, 84, 86, 90** Ann Barrow/Navta Associates, Inc.; **96, 100** Meryl Treatner/Navta Associates, Inc.